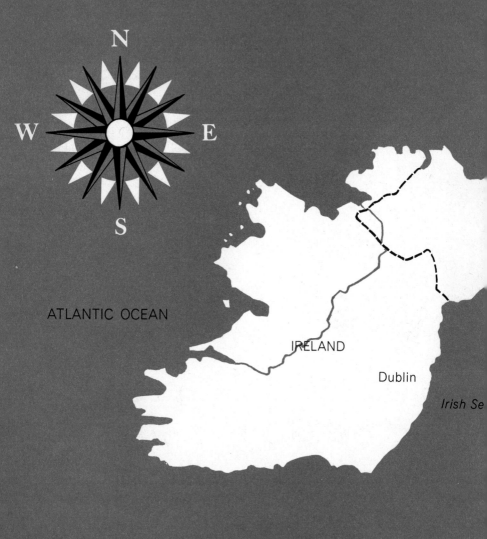

N

W E

S

ATLANTIC OCEAN

IRELAND

Dublin

Irish Se

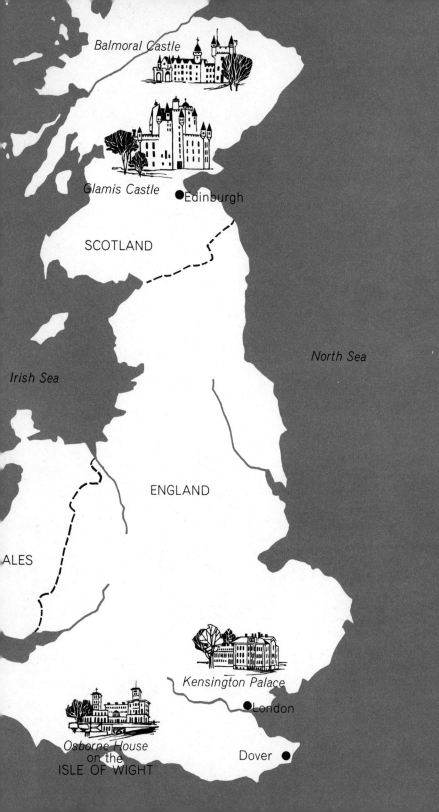

Balmoral Castle

Glamis Castle

●Edinburgh

SCOTLAND

North Sea

Irish Sea

ENGLAND

ALES

Kensington Palace

●London

Osborne House
on the
ISLE OF WIGHT

Dover ●

the true story of

QUEEN VICTORIA

the true story of

QUEEN
VICTORIA

BRITISH MONARCH

BY ARTHUR H. BOOTH

 CHILDRENS PRESS, CHICAGO

American edition published through the courtesy of

Frederick Muller Limited

London

Library of Congress Catalog Card Number: 64-19878

Copyright © in Great Britain, 1961, Arthur H. Booth

© 1964, Childrens Press

Lithographed in the U.S.A.

3 4 5 6 7 8 9 10 11 12 13 14 15 16 17 18 19 20 21 22 23 24 25   R   75 74 73 72 71 70 69 68

Contents

Credits

Designer/BERT RAY STUDIO

Illustrations by/PARVIZ SADIGHIAN

Cover Painting/MARY GEHR

Type/CALEDONIA

Paper/ 70# PUBLISHERS OFFSET

Printer/REGENSTEINER CORPORATION

Author and Artist

Arthur H. Booth has spent all his adult life in British journalism, and is now Chief Reporter for the Press Association, London. During his long career in Fleet Street he has covered most of the important events in recent British history, including many stories of world impact. He has reported on the activities of all the major British statesmen of the past thirty years, and covered the stirring wartime speeches of Churchill. Besides his biographies of Sir Winston Churchill and Queen Victoria, Mr. Booth has written a biography of Sir Christopher Wren and short histories of the French Revolution, the Great Religions of the World, the American Civil War, and the First World War.

Parviz Sadighian was born in Tehran, Iran, in 1939. He was graduated from the Academy of Fine Arts in Tehran and received a partial scholarship for foreign study. In 1959 he enrolled at the Art Institute in Chicago and continued his studies in sculpture and in painting. Interest in painting led to courses in illustration and advertising art. Mr. Sadighian is now associated with the Bert Ray Studio in Chicago.

Foreword

The reign of Queen Victoria, which started when she was still a slim girl in her teens, will always rank as one of the greatest Britain has ever known.

This story traces her life from the convent-like seclusion of her girlhood to the splendors of imperial glory at the close of the long Victorian era. Victoria saw the drama of this exciting time unfold. It was an age of exploration and invention, which brought to the world the marvels of railroad trains, automobiles, telephones, phonographs, cameras, moving pictures, and one of the greatest wonders of all—electricity.

The book gives a lively panorama of the period as well as a penetrating character study of Victoria, who from the start was determined to assert herself as a ruler. The main emphasis is on the earlier part of the reign, before the death of the Prince Consort caused her to go into permanent mourning.

"I will be good."

She was a little girl of twelve, noticeably small for her age, when she made the famous promise. It was her sole comment on realizing for the first time that one day she would be queen.

Combined with almost flaxen hair and large blue eyes set above bulging pink cheeks, her smallness of stature gave her

15

a deceptively doll-like appearance. Yet far from being anything like a mere puppet—at that or at any other age—she was in fact extremely self-willed, with a decided mind of her own. Her mouth was firm as well as tiny; and firmness was the key to her character throughout her life.

Taken out of their royal context—which necessarily involved the daunting prospect of a long career of hard and exacting service as head of the state—the well-known words might seem priggish for a twelve-year-old. But little Victoria was quite serious about it: she made the goody-goody promise with wide-eyed solemnity, free from any trace of either priggishness or sham. She meant it; and she knew what it meant even at that early age.

And she proved true to her word: she became a good queen—very good indeed. Her long reign—due to start, as it happened, when she was still only a girl in her teens—will always rank in history as one of the greatest Britain has ever known. It turned out to be an astonishing period of exploration and invention, full of marvels. Its manifold legacies, some sordid but most of them rich, are with us to this day.

Not so long ago, especially in the uneasy years between the two world wars, nearly everybody thought that it was clever to follow the popular practice of talking with a superior sneer about the Victorians—strange old-fashioned people in frock coats or crinolines, top hats or bonnets and bustles, with acres of stifling velvet and lace for their children. Nowadays we know better than to sneer. On the contrary, we are inclined to give the Victorians a respectful salute whenever we look back on their amazing achievements.

In their memorable epoch of progress, crowded with great adventures of the mind as well as pioneering efforts in many materialistic fields previously unexplored, they transformed the pattern of life throughout the whole world. Britain, the small island realm presided over by an illustrious queen, was the vigorous mainspring of that global revolution.

Later in this book we will see those dazzling years of expansion, but now let us find out why it was that a little girl brought up in cramping seclusion, knowing hardly anything of the lives of ordinary people, was destined even in childhood to succeed to the British throne and thereby give her name to a momentous era of profound change for mankind everywhere.

She was born at the very beginning of the Steam Age. The date was May 24, 1819, and the place was Kensington Palace, which at that time was separated from London by country lanes and market gardens. It was in that very year that George Stephenson, a promising young engineer, had successfully shown for the first time on a track of metal rails —as distinct from an ordinary road—that his new steam locomotive could supply a pulling power beyond the united strength of any team of horses.

The epoch-making demonstration of the first railway took place in a grimy district far removed from the leafy quietude of Kensington; it was staged at Hetton Colliery, in the county of Durham, and as a result of it Stephenson secured a contract for the building of the Stockton and Darlington line, the world's first passenger railroad.

It was not till four years later that the Stockton and Darlington line was opened for public traffic; and it was in that same memorable year of 1823, when Victoria was only four years old, that little Charles Dickens, then aged eleven, was put to work in a London blacking factory to ease the poverty of his parents.

Stephenson and Dickens. In themselves those names seem to epitomize the two greatest achievements of the Victorian era, consisting of marvelous inventions and immortal literature, but there were many other names on the shining roll of honor. In the year of Victoria's birth Tennyson was still at school, but at the Royal Institution not far from Kensington Palace a young laboratory assistant named Michael Faraday was already making preliminary experiments with the mysterious forces of magnetism and electricity.

The royal baby was the only child of the then Duke of Kent, fourth son of George III, but she never knew her father. He died when she was only eight months old—on January 23, 1820—one week before the death of his own aged and mad father, whose demise brought a new reign. George III was succeeded by the eldest son of his large family, the Prince Regent, who became George IV at the age of fifty-eight. As soon as she could talk Victoria always called him "Uncle King."

There were numerous uncles on both sides of her family.

On the paternal side—the all-important one for succession to the crown—none of her late father's three older brothers had legitimate children still alive, and when George IV began his reign she became third in succession to the throne. He was a king notorious for heavy debts and loose living, and as a result of this, monarchy at that time was an unpopular institution in Britain.

Victoria's mother was a well-meaning but quarrelsome woman who dominated the child's early life and never left her side. Before her marriage to the Duke of Kent she had been a widowed princess of the small kingdom of Saxe-Coburg-Gotha, and she could hardly speak English. Nearly all her talks with her daughter were in German, but little Victoria, always bright and alert, soon picked up English as well.

It was a strange and somewhat straitened household at Kensington, neither merry nor wealthy. When he had died so soon after the birth of his only child the Duke of Kent had left little except a large pile of debts. He had chosen only two baptismal names for her—Alexandrina Victoria, the first in honor of the Tsar Alexander I of Russia, who had attended the christening ceremony, and the second because it was also her mother's name.

"Drina," a shortened version of the first of the two names, was what she was always called in the family circle during childhood, but when she eventually succeeded to the throne she promptly chose "Victoria" for official title; she never liked the Russian associations attached to her first name.

Of course she did not remember her father, and the place thus left vacant in her affections was largely occupied by a revered uncle, one of her mother's brothers, who lived in England throughout Victoria's childhood. He later accepted the proffered throne of Belgium and became Leopold I, first ruler of that newly formed kingdom. He had expert knowledge of the intricacies of constitutional monarchy, and as the years went by he had great influence on her.

Another major influence during childhood, by far the greatest of all, was that of her governess, Fräulein Louise Lehzen, daughter of a German pastor, who at the request of George IV was soon created a baroness of Hanover, her native land. Her official title in the household at Kensington was Personal Attendant on the Princess, in which capacity she was responsible for instructions in conduct as well as general education.

It was to Baroness Lehzen that Victoria made the well-known promise quoted at the beginning of this book. On Victoria's twelfth birthday the governess gave her a printed family tree, showing her relation to the throne. After solemnly studying it for a few moments, Victoria said: "Then I shall be queen. I will be good."

The truth of the matter was that up to that time the little girl had often been bad and willful in her conduct. Perhaps the baroness felt that the best way to pull her up and make her better was to show her what destiny had in store. The net result seemed to justify that revealing course of action: thereafter Victoria rapidly improved; she became good.

"Lehzen often said that she never had charge of such a passionate and naughty child as I was," said Victoria on a much later occasion of recalling her early years. "Still, she also said that I never told her a falsehood even if I knew I would be punished for what I had done. I adored her, though I was greatly in awe of her."

And it is pleasant to record here that the adoration, if not the awe, continued throughout the governess's lifetime. When she was an old lady living in retirement in Hanover, at a time when her former pupil had been on the British throne for many years, she regularly received each week a gossipy letter from Buckingham Palace ("With love to dear Lehzen") written in the Queen's own hand.

The fat and gouty King George IV disliked Victoria's mother, whom he regarded as quarrelsome and interfering, but he very much liked his little niece, and she in turn felt that he was quite a charming person. But she was horrified one day when he kissed her; she found that his bloated face was covered with greasepaint to camouflage his pouches and wrinkles. She liked it much better when he merely shook her hand in greeting—a polite action which he invariably preceded with a gruff royal command: "Give us your paw!"

On one visit to Windsor there was a concert in the conservatory and the King asked her to name her favorite tune, so that he could order the band to play it for her. "God Save The King" was her pert reply. He was so delighted that he gave her a miniature of himself set in diamonds.

She always remembered him with affection, despite that dreadful kiss. When he died she was eleven years old, and she did not fully realize what his demise meant to her own prospects. The position then was this: overnight she had become heir presumptive to the throne, next in succession to the new king, another of her uncles, who reigned as William IV. He was the second son of the late George III, and because the third son had died childless three years earlier she was next in line by virtue of the fact that she was the only descendant of the fourth son.

At the time of his accession William IV was sixty-four years old and had no legitimate children of his own; therefore Victoria automatically became heir to the royal title. The provision of adequate tuition for preparing her to fulfil her manifest destiny became a matter of urgent concern to the nation, and Parliament immediately decided to grant to her mother an additional allowance of £10,000 (at that time equal to about $50,000) a year for the upbringing and education of the future monarch.

It was an intensive preparation, not limited to schoolbook subjects. Her program of education was mainly concentrated on languages, history, music, drawing, painting, and deportment. That last item may sound "dated," but in fact it proved to be of the utmost value to Victoria; by strict training she acquired at an early age a regal dignity of carriage that greatly helped in later years to offset her smallness of stature.

Even as an adult she never quite reached five feet in

height, and she was once heard to say, "Everybody grows but me," but because of her early lessons in deportment she always looked a queen whenever she was later called upon to perform public ceremonies. As a girl she was taught to walk correctly and to bow and curtsy with unselfconscious elegance. Sometimes a bunch of prickly holly was pinned beneath her little chin to ensure that she would hold herself erect while walking in the privacy of the rooms of Kensington Palace.

Formal dancing, with instruction given by an expert mistress brought over from Paris, also formed part of the training in deportment. In music she quickly showed genuine good taste, and her fondness for the works of first-class composers —particularly Beethoven, Mozart, Schubert, Verdi—provided an unfailing solace to her in both youth and age. Under the guidance of the organist of St. Margaret's Church, Westminster, she developed a sweet soprano voice.

Each of her tutors was an acknowledged expert in his chosen field. For instance, her art lessons were given by a Royal Academy member, and she soon became accomplished with both pencil and brush, and especially water colors. Sketching remained one of her most cherished hobbies. Hundreds of her drawings, many of them excellent portraits, are to this day carefully stored at Windsor.

One of the masters at Westminster School taught her writing and arithmetic. Her penmanship became extremely fluent, and throughout her life she proved to be a tireless letter writer, as a result of which a vast collection of her correspondence, invaluable to historians for the study of the Victorian period, is still preserved in the royal archives. Though not always showing exactitude in English grammar, those gushing letters, full of underlinings to give emphasis, were invariably written with absolute sincerity and with an impressively accurate eye for even the smallest details of objects or events she wished to describe.

In learning foreign languages she rapidly became completely at home with French and German. Together with her native English, this meant that she was effortlessly tri-lingual—a great asset in the high position for which she was destined. She also acquired a useful working knowledge of Italian.

It was a strict and strenuous life, carefully sheltered from the outside world, and over both work and play her mother kept constant vigilance. Until she was on the threshold of womanhood Victoria always slept in her mother's bedroom. A secluded existence of that sort was regarded as essential among the royal families of Europe at that period—in striking contrast to the happy prep-school upbringing of Prince Charles, heir to the throne nearly a century and a half later.

The summer of 1832, when she was thirteen, brought a welcome if only temporary change from the convent-like seclusion of Kensington Palace. Her mother decided that it was time to take Victoria on a visit to some of the houses of the nobility. Accompanied by Baroness Lehzen and other members of the household, they went on a tour stretching into Wales.

The Princess naturally enjoyed every minute of the journey, made in a private carriage drawn by relays of horses. One important by-product, with lasting consequences, was that at the outset her mother instructed her to keep a journal of the tour, and she presented her with a large notebook for that purpose. It was the beginning of an enduring practice; thereafter, right up to the last week of her long life, Victoria made daily entries in her journals, which were replaced as soon as they were filled and in the end totaled more than a hundred closely written volumes.

At the start Victoria adopted the practice of writing the entries in pencil first of all, so that she could show them to Lehzen for approval before she inked them over for the inspection of her mother. In the earliest diaries the pencil markings can still be detected here and there beneath the ink. Throughout the tour she carefully noted what she saw *en route*, and in that way she soon developed extremely acute powers of observation—a formidable trait for her ministers of later years, one of whom was then heard to say, "Nothing ever escapes her eye."

From the outset she showed an easy mastery of words, quite impressive for a girl her age, though her lively descriptive powers were a little over-colored to begin with. For instance, early in the journey the royal carriage passed through Birmingham and the Black Country, and this is what she noted in her diary:

"We just passed through a town where all the coal mines are, and you see the fire glimmer at a distance in the engines in many places. The men, women, children, country, and houses are all black. The country is very desolate everywhere; there are coals about, and the grass is quite blasted and black. The country continues black, engines flaming, coals in abundance, everywhere smoking and burning coal-heaps, intermingled with wretched huts and carts and little ragged children."

Victoria's liking for travel and her zest for noting everything she saw are immediately apparent in the pages of her journal. Those two characteristics continued throughout life; they can be found from start to finish in all the many volumes she filled.

Back at Kensington after the tour, she untiringly maintained the practice of keeping a diary. By the following year, under the date May 24, she was to be found solemnly penning this entry: "Today is my birthday. I am fourteen years old! How very *old!*"

Always an early riser, she was even earlier than usual that bright morning; she was wide awake by 5:30 a.m. In her journal she later listed the numerous presents she received. They included a brooch from her mother and "a pretty little china figure and a lovely little china basket" from "dear Lehzen."

Another tour was made that summer. It stretched as far west as Plymouth, with a visit to Portsmouth to see H.M.S. *Victory* and the spot where Nelson fell, together with a trip to the Isle of Wight, where for the first time she went to Osborne. She was entranced by that part of the island, which was going to have an important place in her affections during the decades ahead.

In the next year, when she was fifteen, there was not only a summer tour—Yorkshire on that occasion—but also a visit to Ascot races, where she was given a prominent place in the royal procession down the course and was loudly cheered by the crowd.

Outside the royal family and a limited circle of the upper nobility, few people really knew much about the Princess, but King William IV was among the first to recognize that she was rapidly becoming highly popular. As a young man he had served in the Royal Navy, and one day when he was discussing Victoria with a friend he made this true comment about her future:

"It will touch every sailor's heart to have a girl queen to fight for. They'll be tattooing her face on their arms, and I'll be bound they'll all think she was christened after Nelson's ship."

A New Reign

On her sixteenth birthday, which she celebrated at Kensington Palace on May 24, 1835, Victoria demurely noted in her journal that she had at last begun to appreciate her lessons and hoped thereafter to make good progress. She also wrote: "I feel that the two years to come till I attain my eighteenth are the most important of any almost."

It was a significant comment. It disclosed that she fully

realized the uniqueness of her position under the British constitution, which in relation to the monarchy provides that any heir to the throne, whether boy or girl, attains his or her so-called "majority" not on becoming twenty-one but at the age of eighteen.

Her mother had already been nominated by Parliament as potential regent in the event of the death of King William before that official coming-of-age by his heir, but if the King lived on till after that period then Victoria would automatically ascend the throne at his death with full constitutional rights as queen, without any interim of a regency.

Victoria's hopes that she would make good progress with her lessons were well founded. Although decidedly not an "intellectual," she was painstakingly studious, and she quickly acquired a varied store of knowledge in subjects likely to be useful to her during the years ahead.

Wide rather than deep, her learning was nevertheless by no means superficial. Most important of all—as her journal occasionally disclosed in her comments on other people—she was clearly developing a keen and accurate eye for qualities of character, good or bad, in the persons she met.

"A very old person I am indeed!" was one of the diary entries on her seventeenth birthday, which was forever memorable to her because one of the visitors to Kensington on that occasion included for the first time a fascinating cousin of hers, Prince Albert of Saxe-Coburg-Gotha, whose father, the reigning Duke of that minor State in Germany, was her mother's eldest brother. Albert, just three months younger than she was, delighted Victoria with his lively company.

"Extremely handsome, very clever and intelligent," was her verdict on him.

Of course she did not tell him so to his face; she confided that glowing opinion to the pages of her private journal, which also contained this first impression of him: "His eyes are large and blue, and he has a beautiful nose and a very sweet mouth with fine teeth, but the charm of his countenance is his expression, which is most delightful."

During Albert's stay at Kensington she found that his accomplishments included music and drawing, in both of which he was adept. She often sang to his accompaniments at the piano, and they sketched together in the grounds of the palace. Quite evidently she was deeply attracted to him; and she was happy at the prospects opening before her.

In a letter to Leopold—by then resident in Brussels as King of the Belgians—she wrote immediately after the visit:

I must thank you, my beloved Uncle, for the prospect of great happiness you have contributed to give in the person of dear Albert . . . He possesses every quality that could be desired to render me perfectly happy.

When the time came for Prince Albert to leave Kensington she cried—"very bitterly," as she confided to her diary.

In many ways they were admirably suited to each other. They possessed numerous traits in common, not least of which was their joint enthusiasm for being fully occupied in their leisure hours. In several pages of her diary she again and again expressed that characteristic. One typical passage said: "I love to be employed; I hate to be idle."

It was the same with Albert, whose upbringing in childhood had been even more strenuous than hers. His education from the age of six onward had been carried out to a strict timetable, with a specified number of hours given to lessons every day, increasing in daily duration with the passing of each year. Soon after the visit to Kensington he became a student at the University of Bonn, where his diligence earned high praise from tutors.

King Leopold had been taking an increasing interest in her future. Almost every week letters passed between them. On his side the correspondence was full of guidance on the problems that would inevitably face her on ascending the throne, whenever that time might come, and to help her in making decisions he sent to Kensington his own confidential adviser, Baron Christian Stockmar.

Behind the scenes the Baron's services proved to be invaluable. In Coburg he had practiced as a physician till he had turned his talents to statecraft, and for years he had acted as Leopold's private agent in delicate negotiations affecting constitutional affairs.

From the start Victoria found that she could place complete reliance on Baron Stockmar, who had a decisive influence on her course of conduct at this critical stage.

Both her eighteenth birthday and the declining condition of King William's health had made Victoria acutely conscious of the great yet anxious prospect rapidly looming nearer. In her journal on the birthday she made this solemn vow:

I shall from this day take the firm resolution to study with renewed assiduity, to keep my attention always well fixed on whatever I am about, and to strive to become every day less trifling and more fit for what, if Heaven wills, I am some day to be.

Within little more than one month the death of William IV brought the fulfilment of "what, if Heaven wills, I am some day to be." On the fifteenth of June she learned that "my poor uncle the King" was so ill that his doctors feared he would live only a few days longer. The news from Windsor, where the King lay, grew increasingly bad, and on the nineteenth she was told that he could hardly live through that day.

In fact, he died shortly after 2:00 a.m. on the twentieth, and on that memorable morning Victoria was awakened by her mother at six o'clock to be told that the Archbishop of Canterbury and the Lord Chamberlain were waiting to see her. They wished to have audience with her alone, without the presence of her mother or anyone else.

Victoria immediately realized why they were there; she knew they had come to tell her that she was queen. Thus it was that her reign, destined to be the longest in either English or British history—both before and after the union with Scotland—began on June 20, 1837.

The two waiting men, of long experience in affairs of state, provided a striking contrast to the girl queen, a slim and modest figure clad only in a nightdress, a cotton dressing gown, and a shawl, which, together with her slippers, she had hurriedly put on as she had gotten out of bed to enter her sitting room. They bowed low.

The Archbishop, Dr. William Howley, was seventy-one years of age. He was so old-fashioned that he still wore a wig—the last man in his high office to retain that eighteenth-century practice. He looked even older than his years. He had been a prelate before Victoria was born; his promotion to Canterbury in 1828 had been preceded by fifteen years as Bishop of London.

The Lord Chamberlain, Lord Conyngham, was forty-one. By virtue of his position as chief officer of the royal household he was responsible for organizing all great occasions of state—accessions, coronations, and royal funerals. As Victoria approached he humbly knelt in homage and gravely kissed her hand. It was he who told her the sad news from Windsor while he still knelt before her.

Both men had been at the bedside of the dying King. As swiftly as possible they had traveled by carriage during the early hours in order to announce in person to Victoria her accession to the throne. After Lord Conyngham had made the formal announcement, the Archbishop described to her the King's last hours and told her that in the closing phase he had "directed his mind to religion" and had died happy.

Victoria's first thought was for the widowed Queen Adelaide. She at once instructed Lord Conyngham to express to her "my feelings of condolence and sorrow." It was her first royal command and the Lord Chamberlain immediately returned to Windsor to carry it out. The Archbishop left with him, though to drive to his palace at Lambeth, not back to Windsor.

When they had gone Victoria joined her mother and Baroness Lehzen, who had been waiting outside the door of the sitting room. She wept on her mother's shoulder, and, with the sufferings of the late King still in her mind, she said, "He was always so very, very kind to me." In her diary that morning she wrote:

Since it has pleased Providence to place me in this station, I shall do my utmost to fulfil my duty towards my country. I am very young, and perhaps in many, though not in all things, inexperienced, but I am sure that very few have more real good will and more real desire to do what is fit and right than I have.

At breakfast "the good and faithful Stockmar," as she called him in her diary, came to talk to her. He was full of tactful advice on the question of how best to conduct herself during the rest of that momentous day, the arrangements for which included the holding of an "accession" meeting of the Privy Council to swear loyalty to the new monarch.

No sooner was breakfast finished than a messenger brought a letter from the Prime Minister, Viscount Melbourne, announcing that he would do "himself the honor of waiting upon your Majesty a little before nine this morning."

Viscount Melbourne, in full court dress of velvet coat, knee breeches, and buckled shoes, was prompt in his arrival. It was not their first meeting; she had seen him a few times before, especially at royal banquets at Windsor, but until that morning she had never had the opportunity of talking to him alone. From the outset she was entranced; she found that her Prime Minister, very much a man of the world, was not merely a most dependable official adviser but was also a delightful companion whose witty conversation never failed to fascinate her.

Of all the inner group who proved to have great influence on Victoria during the early part of the reign, Viscount Melbourne henceforth had to be ranked as highest on the list—higher even than Uncle Leopold or Baron Stockmar. It was as though some shining star of first magnitude, hitherto glimpsed only occasionally at a remote distance in outer space, had suddenly swung right into her orbit.

Melbourne dazzled her. He in turn found that in this final phase of his long public career he had encountered an entirely new interest that utterly and joyfully absorbed his time and attention, to the exclusion of everything else. He was sincerely happy to serve his new monarch and to place at her disposal all his accomplishments, all his vast experience of men and affairs, in order that the opening years of her reign should be made smooth and successful. Her welfare became the sole interest of his life.

He at once felt that she relied on him in much the same way as she would have relied upon a father—the father she had never known. His response to that trust was immediate, generous, and unstinting.

Evidently she had made up her mind on some matters some time before the accession. When Melbourne knelt and kissed her hand preliminary to the first audience she at once told him that it had "long been my intention" to retain him and the rest of the existing ministry at the head of governmental affairs.

Before going to Kensington he had written out for her, in his own handwriting, the formal declaration which she would have to make to the Privy Council. She agreed with him that the meeting of the council should be held as soon as possible. He suggested 11:30 a.m., and she consented.

Lord Melbourne left to make the necessary arrangements. By that time a large crowd had collected outside Kensington Palace. Naturally there was general regret at King William's death, news of which had by then spread throughout London, but there was also an unmistakable feeling of high expectancy, almost of joy, mixed with the sorrow. Quite obviously the new reign would be totally different from any that had been known within the memory of anyone then living.

The opening ceremonies of the reign were performed by Victoria with polished elegance and regal dignity. Her calm self-assurance astonished everybody privileged to be present at those inaugural occasions.

First, there was the Accession Council. It was held in the largest room of Kensington Palace, known as the Red Saloon because of the wall color. Leaders of church and state, many of them white-haired men with names famous throughout the land, were obsequiously awaiting her as she entered the saloon and gracefully moved forward to her chair.

While the bowing privy councilors stood in an attentive semicircle, she remained seated—a small and lonely but by no means pathetic figure dressed in deep mourning for the late King. In clear and firm tones, attractively modulated, she read the Declaration of Accession prepared by Lord Melbourne, whose admiration for her was enhanced by the accomplished manner in which she performed that first semi-public duty.

Each man advanced in turn and knelt momentarily before her to be sworn in as a member of her council—"Her Majesty's Most Honourable Privy Council," as it was officially called, membership of which carried the prefix "Right Honourable." After the ceremony she left the saloon with the same queenly dignity that she had shown on entering.

All the councilors were deeply impressed, not least the Duke of Wellington. Sixty-eight years old at that time, the Iron Duke was still the nation's greatest hero, despite some unpopular measures that had been passed into law when he had been Prime Minister a few years earlier. Describing the Queen's graceful conduct at her first council, he afterward told a friend that if she had been his own daughter he could not have wished to see her perform the part better.

"I was not at all nervous," she wrote in her diary. She added this modest understatement of the impression she had made: "I had the satisfaction of hearing that people were satisfied with what I had done and how I had done it."

At that first council one significant feature, operative thereafter throughout the reign, was that she had signed the register "Victoria," even though the documents already prepared for subsequent publication had described her as "Alexandrina Victoria." At her own request the first name was withdrawn, and she firmly explained that she always wished to be known solely as "Victoria."

On the first evening of her reign, still at Kensington Palace, she decided to dine alone in an upstairs room, and she told her mother that henceforth she must insist on having a bedroom of her own. From the outset the Duchess of Kent —who must have felt neglected, perhaps slighted—was made to realize that her daughter intended to act independently now that she was queen.

There was sound purpose, beneficial to the state, behind Victoria's apparently aloof and somewhat unfilial attitude. She had noticed in the past, with those sharp and well-trained eyes of hers, that her mother's circle of friends and advisers included several detestable intriguers who for their own ends had often attempted to influence court affairs, sometimes with success. Victoria was determined never to allow such practices under her own regime.

In particular, she strongly disapproved of Sir John Conroy, the comptroller of the Duchess's official household, and it was because of the firm steps she took from the beginning of the reign that he lost power at court. In truth, he was unpleasant and unreliable—an intriguer whose influence on her mother's affairs had helped no one except himself and had often caused ill feeling at Windsor in the days of the late King William.

Thus it was already clear that at the relatively early age of eighteen the Queen could be ruthless as well as charming, once her mind was made up on any issue. Her personal qualities contained more than a mere streak of iron; at times she could be as unyielding—and as cold—as solid steel.

The lonely childhood, spent mainly among grown-up women instead of playmates of her own age, had caused her to develop cool and detached powers of self-reliance which proved to be of immense value in the new circumstances. On occasion she could be hard and imperious—qualities not unbecoming a queen.

Official proclamations of the beginning of the new reign were made in various parts of the land on the day after the accession, with the chief ceremony in the courtyard of St. James's Palace. Trumpeters and heralds in their traditional uniforms stood on the ramparts, and the colorful scene was watched from a window by Victoria. Immediately afterward she gave an audience to the Earl Marshal for the purpose of deciding on arrangements for the late King's funeral. It was held at Windsor a few days later.

Thereafter came a rapid succession of further ceremonies, at all of which the Queen conducted herself with gracious dignity, highly commended by all beholders. One of the witnesses, Princess Lieven, was exceptionally well versed in the etiquette of court life because of her position as wife of the Russian ambassador in London. Describing the Queen, she said in a letter to a friend:

She possesses a composure, an air of command and of dignity, which, with her childlike face, her tiny figure, and her pretty smile, create one of the most extraordinary impressions that it is possible to imagine.

Princess Lieven also found that in private conversation Victoria was "extremely reserved," and she decided that "prudence is one of her highest qualities." In acquiring that discreet trait Victoria had been helped by Uncle Leopold, who in one of his instructive letters said:

All trades must be learned, and nowadays the trade of a constitutional Sovereign, to do it well, is a very difficult one.

Because of her experience in various courts of Europe, in addition to London and St. Petersburg, Princess Lieven was an expert on the difficult "trade" of royalty. Another expert opinion on one of the Queen's attractive qualities—her alluring voice—came from Miss Fanny Kemble, the leading actress of the period. Miss Kemble was famous for her appearances in Shakespearean roles, especially Juliet and Ophelia.

"Her voice is exquisite," said Miss Kemble. "The enuncia-

43

tion is as perfect as the intonation is melodious. It is impossible to hear a more excellent utterance than that of the Queen's English by the English Queen."

The occasion which caused Miss Kemble to form that high opinion was a speech dissolving Parliament on July 17, 1837, less than a month after the beginning of the reign. In those days a general election automatically followed the demise of the monarch. In accordance with constitutional practice Victoria went to the House of Lords to perform the ceremony of bringing the existing Parliament to a close.

On arrival she went to a dressing-room to put on her royal robe of crimson velvet, which she found to be "enormously heavy." Lord Melbourne, bearing the Sword of State, immediately preceded her as she entered the Lords' Chamber, and he stood at her left when she was seated on the throne. In her diary that night she said:

I feel always a satisfaction to have him near me on such occasions, as he is such an honest, good, kind-hearted man and is my friend, I know it.

She also recalled that she had "felt somewhat (but very little) nervous" before reading the speech. Nevertheless, "it did very well, and I was happy to hear that people were satisfied." Next day she wrote to King Leopold describing the scene and telling him that she was "not at all tired today, but quite frisky."

The correspondence between them was becoming voluminous, particularly from his side; he was determined to place at her disposal his immense store of worldly wisdom. Dealing with the question of being reserved in conversation, Leopold said in one of his letters that he had heard there were "many intrigues on foot in England at this moment," and he gave this advice:

A rule which I cannot sufficiently recommend is, never to permit people to speak on subjects concerning yourself or your affairs without your having yourself desired them to do so. The moment a person behaves improperly on this subject, change the conversation and make the individual feel that he has made a mistake.

That letter was sent to an entirely new address: Buckingham Palace. The move had taken place four days before the dissolution of Parliament. Victoria was the first British monarch to use Buckingham Palace as an official residence, and although she was pleased with the larger quarters, much less cramped than Kensington, she never really liked the new home.

Originally built for the Dukes of Buckingham, it had been bought by George III in 1762, but neither he nor any of his sons had lived there, despite the fact that both George IV and William IV had ordered extensive reconstruction, intending to use it as the chief royal residence in London. Incidentally, the outer form of Buckingham Palace as it is today is not the one that Victoria knew; the existing façade was not added until 1913, in the reign of George V.

In her diary the Queen described her own rooms as "high, pleasant and cheerful," but she soon found that the huge palace was by no means completely ready for occupation. Baroness Lehzen was given a sitting room next to her suite. By contrast, her mother's apartments were in a distant wing— quite comfortable, but definitely detached from Victoria.

A week after the move the Queen held a levee, the first of many in the reign; St. James's Palace, which she still favored for the most ceremonial occasions, was chosen for it. Many men who had been awarded official appointments of various sorts, either in Britain or the colonies, were presented to her. Each knelt to kiss her hand, and that evening she made this exclamatory comment in her diary: "I had my hand kissed nearly 3,000 times!"

One personal shortcoming that slightly worried Victoria was that she was out of practice in horseback riding. She therefore decided that she could not risk holding a formal review of her troops, as was customary for a new monarch, until she had remedied that defect.

As a little girl she had often ridden a favorite pony named Rosa. Now, in the large riding school attached to the stables at Buckingham Palace, she practiced on various mounts almost daily for several weeks until she became an accomplished horsewoman. Fondness for animals, particularly horses and dogs, was one of her characteristics. Her greatest pet, a spaniel named Dash, had belonged to her mother.

By autumn she was able to stage a review at Windsor. She took the salute sitting sidesaddle on a horse called Leopold. Her riding habit for that glittering occasion was a semi-uniform of navy blue, with scarlet collar and cuffs and a wide skirt. She also wore the blue sash and silver star of the Order of the Garter, and on her head was a military cap fastened beneath her chin with a golden strap.

"I felt for the first time like a man, as if I could myself fight at the head of my troops," she wrote in her journal. The review was a brilliant success, and the glowing reports of it published in the newspapers added to the increasing popularity of the new Queen.

She became a dashing horsewoman, fond of galloping in Windsor Great Park, with the court riding behind her. Every day on such occasions her chief companion was Lord Melbourne, whose sparkling conversation as he rode at her side never failed to enthrall her.

Lord Melbourne's growing popularity with the Queen was resented by his political opponents at Westminster, where he was head of the Whig Party. Leaders of the Tories, the official opposition, suspected that because of his influence Victoria was becoming far too partial in her approach to political questions. He continued as Prime Minister while the general election campaign—a process prolonged over many weeks—was still in progress, and the Tory fears about the attitude of the palace toward Westminster were not without substance; it was true that Victoria wanted the Whigs to win.

"I'm somewhat anxious about the elections," she confessed in her journal. "I trust in Heaven that we shall have a majority for us and that the present Government may remain firm for long."

Of course she should not have shown such favoritism, especially in alluding to the Whigs as "us," but she naturally placed great reliance on Lord Melbourne and would have felt almost lost if she had been deprived of his services as Prime Minister. In excuse it must be remembered that she was still quite young and relatively inexperienced.

Furthermore, the crown was not at that time as aloof from party politics as it later became. This now traditional aloofness was largely brought about during the reign of Victoria as she learned more and more about national problems. Lord Melbourne himself did not hesitate to point out to her that there was an official opposition, the members of which might supplant the Whig Government at any time.

He was always utterly correct in his attitude, as the Duke of Wellington, the most forceful of the Tories, ungrudgingly admitted. In fact there could have been no better man than Melbourne as the Queen's first tutor in the intricacies of politics. He never took party advantage of the fact that she placed the utmost trust in him; he never forgot that she was the sovereign and therefore should not be involved too deeply in party squabbles on either side.

Their talks together ranged over many subjects, not merely constitutional matters, and she never tired of putting questions to him to get his views on a wide variety of topics, including even such problems as what books she ought to read. Conscious of her almost ceaseless questioning, she timidly told him one day that she thought she was often very childish and stupid in her conversation and must sometimes bore him with her tiresome questions.

"Never the least," he replied. "You *ought* to ask." Allaying her fears that she was often childish in her talk, he said, "You've no reason to think that."

The results of the election declared in the autumn made little difference to the strength of the parties at Westminster, and the Queen was greatly relieved to find that Lord Melbourne could command sufficient support in both Houses for him to continue as Prime Minister. He cheerfully set about the task of preparing a speech for her to read at the opening of the new Parliament containing proposed legislation for the session due to be held during the winter.

His return to power was a source of intense satisfaction to Victoria, who felt that it put a seal of happiness on the first few months of the reign. She decided that she thoroughly enjoyed being queen, and in her journal she described the weeks she had spent at Windsor as "the pleasantest summer I ever passed in my life."

Every moment of her time had been occupied. Even when Parliament had been in dissolution she had found that the stream of official documents requiring her personal attention never ceased, but she enjoyed performing all the many duties placed upon her.

"I *delight* in this work," she wrote. "I have *so many* communications from ministers, and from me to them, and I get so many papers to sign *every* day that I have always a *very great* deal to do."

Often she underlined words for the purpose of giving them emphasis. That practice, so frequently apparent in her journal, was also to be found in her written instructions to ministers; throughout her life and in all her messages and letters she could never resist displaying that somewhat gushing literary trait, which she had largely derived from her Uncle Leopold, whose own letters contained much underlining of key words.

The new Parliament was opened by her on November 20, 1837, the first of many similar ceremonies during the reign. Clad in her royal robe of crimson, she went to the House of Lords to read her speech from the throne. In front of her were the peers and at the rear of the chamber stood members of the Commons.

Prominent among them was Sir Robert Peel, leader of the Tories in the lower House. Three years before her accession he had been Prime Minister for a brief period while his party was momentarily in power. He disliked some of the proposals contained in the speech but he could not fail to notice that the Queen's reading of it was flawless, and once more the assembled leaders of the land were impressed by her regal bearing and attractive voice.

The concluding part of the speech contained a reference to her own youth and her reliance on the loyalty of her people. It was a personal passage that deeply affected all hearers, not least Lord Melbourne, who had suggested it. Again he stood near her as he proudly bore aloft the Sword of State.

"Good kind Melbourne was quite touched to tears after I read the speech," wrote Victoria in her diary that night. It had been another happy day for her as well as for him, and she felt that the contents of the speech were "excellent."

The session thus opened passed off "very satisfactorily," as she told King Leopold in a letter written to him from Buckingham Palace on Christmas day. She faced the coming of the New Year with confidence and with the knowledge that she had admirably fulfilled all her revered uncle's highest hopes.

Crowning Glory

As leading lady on the great stage of public affairs, Victoria had filled her exacting role with unqualified success thus far. Only a few months earlier she had been almost unknown to the British people; yet by 1838, her coronation year, she was the admired focus of world-wide attention. It had been a remarkable transformation, and she was enjoying every minute of it.

Victoria's emergence from the seclusion of Kensington Palace into the dazzling limelight of the throne could be described in some respects as a Cinderella story. During girlhood she had been relatively poor, allowed only a small amount of pocket money because of the cramped circumstances of the debt-ridden household. Suddenly she found herself rich—enormously rich as time went on.

By wise investments and careful management of her official income — businesslike traits that became even more apparent when at length she got married — she eventually became very wealthy indeed. Royal wills are never published, but when at last the reign ended, financial experts estimated the total value of her estate at about £2,000,000.

In the opening session of the new Parliament the annual sum voted to the Queen was £385,000, an allowance in her own right which was never varied in any succeeding year; but additional grants were made annually by Parliament to her husband, when she married, and to her children when each was born.

Furthermore, she received from the outset the very considerable revenues of the Duchy of Lancaster and the Duchy of Cornwall, two rich sources of income which contained wealthy properties in various parts of the land. The income from the Duchy of Lancaster remained with her throughout life, but the revenues from the Duchy of Cornwall, traditionally intended for the Prince of Wales, automatically passed to her eldest son when he was born. The Cornwall income accrued to her for nearly five years.

Because of the upward trend in the value of landed property, the yields from both those duchies were on an increasing scale during the periods she received them. To begin with they were each worth about £30,000 annually, but in later years the Duchy of Lancaster was itself bringing in £60,000.

From the figures given, it will be seen that the Queen's gross income at the start of the reign was about £445,000 a year—at a time when money values were at least five times greater than they are today. That large income was offset by many inescapable expenses, some of them extremely high.

For example, the annual expenses of the royal household totaled £172,000 from the outset, and in addition the Queen paid £131,000 each year in salaries. It was estimated in 1838 that after defraying necessary and official expenses she had approximately £70,000 a year of her own.

It was characteristic of Victoria, always transparently honest in both word and deed, that as soon as Parliament had announced the size of the allowance to be given her annually—technically known as the Civil List—she decided to pay off her father's debts, totaling £50,000, together with the interest that had been mounting up during the preceding seventeen years. The creditors were delighted, and no doubt many of them were surprised as well, though there would have been no surprise among any of them if they had had the privilege beforehand of knowing her sterling character.

At her relatively girlish age on ascending the throne the Queen was naturally interested in finery, but she was never extravagant in dress, and although her wardrobe had to be enormously expanded she was quite modest in her expenditure in that direction. During the first ten years of the reign she spent an average of just under £4,000 a year on clothes. Thereafter the totals rarely exceeded £4,000 a year, despite rising costs of materials and startling changes in fashions.

The largest dress bill during the first ten years of the reign was incurred in 1840, the year of marriage. In 1838 there had been much talk of a suitable husband, but Lord Melbourne, unlike Uncle Leopold, thought there was no need for an early marriage. The Queen shared her Prime Minister's opinion on that subject.

In truth, Victoria was enjoying so much the early phase of the reign—bringing, as it did, a delightful sense of independence from the bondage of the family ties she had known at Kensington—that she was in no hurry to embark on matrimony. Yet she still had Prince Albert very much in mind—to such an extent that she arranged for Baron Stockmar to go to Coburg for the purpose of supervising Albert's education in statecraft and the "difficult trade," as her uncle had rightly called it, of constitutional monarchy.

That arrangement had the enthusiastic support of Leopold, who was not only eager for the dynastic union of his niece and nephew but was also anxious that such a marriage should be entirely successful politically. He said in a letter to the Queen:

It is my great anxiety to see Albert a very good and distinguished young man, and no pains will be thought too much on my part if this end can be attained.

As part of a carefully prepared program for broadening his outlook on the world, Baron Stockmar accompanied Albert on an educational tour of Italy. By that time Victoria was enjoying immensely her new life of freedom and service. Her chief recreation was horseback riding, to the secret concern of Lord Melbourne, who feared that she might injure herself in a fall.

Rarely a day passed without her being out for at least three hours on one of the numerous mounts, all of them handsome and high spirited kept in the royal mews at Buckingham Palace and Windsor. Often she went far afield—near to such places as Harrow or Ealing, then little more than villages separated from London by miles of unspoiled countryside.

Dancing was another much-favored recreation, and sometimes at royal balls Victoria stayed up till the early hours. She was especially fond of quadrilles. The theater, particularly Drury Lane for Shakespearian performances, was another source of enjoyment.

Literature was another topic they often discussed during interludes of state business. In girlhood the books given to Victoria had been mostly theological, forbiddingly heavy in both content and style, including collections of sermons by eminent preachers, but in January of 1838 she ventured into

what was new literary ground for her by reading fiction—
Scott's *The Bride of Lammermoor,* a current best-seller.

It was the first novel she had ever read. Lord Melbourne
made a somewhat damping comment—"It's very melancholy"
—when he saw her reading it. As a substitute he recommended
several of Scott's other novels which had not long been published, among them *Old Mortality* and *Quentin Durward.*

During this period of Victoria s first introduction to the
fascination of great fiction Charles Dickens was suddenly
leaping into fame. His *Pickwick Papers* had already appeared, and *Oliver Twist* was being serialized in monthly
installments. Not until it had been published in book form
did the Queen decide to read it.

She at once found herself enthralled by that grim yet gay
story of lives so different from her own: the hungry workhouse boy; the gang of pickpockets led by the Artful Dodger;
the thieves' kitchen presided over by Fagin; the burglar Bill
Sikes; and all the rest of that amazing portrait gallery, then
fresh from the printing press. She enthusiastically urged Lord
Melbourne to read *Oliver Twist.* He said, "I will, one day."

It was an exciting period of revolutionary science as well
as immortal literature, though steam locomotion and electricity, the two major triumphs of the reign, were in their
infancy, and as yet Victoria did not dream of ever entrusting
herself to one of the new railroad trains. She had been told
that when the trains were traveling at top speed they could
not be stopped under a distance of 150 yards. It was a shud-
dering thought—to her and to millions of her subjects.

"These steam carriages are very dangerous," she said to Lord Melbourne one day in April of 1838. He heartily concurred, and he complained that "none of these modern inventions considers human life." Nevertheless he had already invested £1,500 of his own money in one of the new railway companies. Britain was on the threshold of the first railway "mania," in which big fortunes were either won or lost—mostly won—by companies mushrooming in various localities.

It was during that same year of 1838 that Faraday announced his momentous discovery of the relationship between the forces of electricity and magnetism. An entry in the Queen's diary recording one of her numerous conversations with Lord Melbourne said:

We spoke about magnetism, which everybody is mad about now. I said it was very disagreeable to be magnetized, as people got to say such odd things in this magnetic state.

To that naive comment by his Queen, the Prime Minister made this shrewd reply: "People say odd enough things without being magnetized."

But the most exciting subject they discussed in the spring of 1838 was neither magnetism nor railways; the recurring focal point of their talks was the forthcoming coronation, which on his recommendation was fixed for June 28. Under Melbourne's leadership the government was determined to make that approaching ceremony in Westminster Abbey a pageant of unparalleled splendor, and they decided to spend on it far more than the £50,000 allocated for the coronation of William IV.

Gorgeous drapings of crimson and gold were ordered for the interior of the Abbey, and it was decided that there should be a new crown because the massive Crown of St. Edward used at earlier coronations was far too heavy for the Queen to wear during the long period after the crowning when she would receive the homage of the procession of peers.

The court jewelers were instructed to make what is now known as the Imperial State Crown, today worn by Queen Elizabeth II whenever she opens Parliament. Victoria was the first monarch to wear it. In brilliance it eclipsed St. Edward's Crown, despite the fact that it weighed only two pounds eleven ounces, compared with five pounds. More than six thousand gems—diamonds, sapphires, emeralds, rubies—made it by far the most dazzling article in all the royal regalia.

Another additional item was a new coronation ring, called "The Wedding Ring of England," for placing on her little finger as a symbol of lifelong service to the state. The previous ring, worn by monarchs since the Restoration under Charles II, was far too big for Victoria.

In connection with the new ring a painful piece of bungling was committed during the coronation by Archbishop Howley, who in advancing age was becoming tottery and slow witted. The underlying trouble was that although everybody had been eagerly discussing the coronation for weeks beforehand, no rehearsal had been held; in consequence of this several mistakes were made in the prolonged service when at last it took place on a pleasant day of summer sunshine.

Early morning showers preceded the sun, but the rain had no dampening effect on the many thousands who had encamped all night along the processional route. In addition to the vast assemblage of Londoners, at least 400,000 people flocked to the capital from many other towns and cities. Only a relative handful, two thousand privileged ticket holders, had places inside the Abbey, which was crammed long before the ceremony started.

Robed peers, carrying their coronets in their hands, were ranged in the north transept in the order of their rank, with dukes at the front and barons in the rear; they were faced by their wives in the south transept. Many of the peeresses, also robed and carrying their coronets, were wearing diamond necklaces that glowed and flashed in the candlelight of the Abbey.

Between those titled representatives of the higher ranks of the realm, on a spacious dais specially erected in front of the chancel, was the old and battered Coronation Chair and the newer and more ornate Chair of Homage. Approached by a short flight of steps, the wooden dais, covered with a rich carpet of purple and gold, was raised five feet above the stone floor.

Victoria made the journey from Buckingham Palace in a gilded coach surmounted by a large scale model of the crown and drawn by eight cream-colored horses. She was wildly cheered along every inch of the decorated route— Constitution Hill, Piccadilly, St. James's Street, Pall Mall, Cockspur Street, Trafalgar Square, Whitehall, and Parliament Street.

At that period Trafalgar Square was being laid out as a memorial to Nelson, a vast scheme of reconstruction which was not completed until 1867. The building work there was smothered in huge flags and drapings of purple and gold— as indeed was every yard of the route. On decorations alone a total of about £200,000 was spent, some by the government but mostly by enthusiastic private citizens.

The triumphal journey, with Yeomen of the Guard from the Tower of London proudly marching beside the coach, lasted an hour and a half: the Queen set out from the Palace at ten o'clock in the morning and did not reach the Abbey until eleven thirty. Such crowds and such cheering had never been seen or heard at any coronation in British history.

Eight young ladies, members of titled families, were dressed in gowns of white satin and silver tissue; they acted as Victoria's attendants from the moment she arrived. On her head was a circlet of diamonds, and she was wearing her velvet robe of state, crimson with trimmings of ermine. The twelve-foot-long train was held by page boys dressed in blue velvet jackets, white kneebreeches and silver-buckled shoes.

Unlike one or two of their elders participating in various phases of the ceremony, the page boys performed their tasks flawlessly—and they were by no means easy, particularly when they were bearing the heavy train in perfect unison while the Queen was turning to left or right at different stages of the service.

"My young trainbearers were always near me and helped me whenever I wanted anything," she said afterward.

In strict privacy on the day before, Victoria had gone to the Abbey to admire the decorated interior and make a general survey of the arrangements, and she had written in her diary that she was glad she had paid that visit because she had thereby learned "exactly where I'm to go." However, because no attempt had then been made to rehearse the proceedings several of the participants, especially the Archbishop of Canterbury, were not familiar with the parts they had to play in the intricate ceremony.

The long and complicated ritual lasted nearly five hours; during the whole time Victoria conducted herself with faultless elegance and dignity. By tradition, maintained to this present day, the ceremony was divided into six distinctive phases: (1) the Recognition; (2) the Oath by the monarch; (3) the Anointing; (4) the Investing; (5) the Crowning; (6) the Homage.

In 1838 the most thrilling part of all was perhaps the first. With tumultuous cries of "God save Queen Victoria!" amidst the shrill blare of trumpets and the rolling crash of drums, the vast congregation enthusiastically acclaimed, or "recognized," the new monarch in response to this question put four times by the Archbishop as he stood on the dais and faced north, south, east, and west, in turn:

Sirs, I here present unto you Queen Victoria, the undoubted Queen of this realm; wherefore, all you who are come this day to do your homage, are you willing to do the same?

After taking her oath of lifelong service to the state, delivered in the clear and alluring voice with which ministers and peers were already familiar, Victoria kissed a Bible held by the Archbishop. The anointing with holy oil on head and hands was also performed by him, as was the investing with the various items of regalia, among them the orb of gold (representing royal dominion) and the golden scepter (symbol of sovereignty).

Another of the insignia used at the investing was the ring, which the Archbishop blunderingly forced on the third finger, instead of the little finger for which it was made. The Primate's mistake caused her "great pain"—as she feelingly wrote afterward—but no murmur of complaint escaped her at the time. In the robing room of the Abbey, when the ceremony was at last over, she found much difficulty in removing the ring from the swollen finger, and she had to bathe her hand in iced water for that painful purpose.

The Archbishop's lapse from the rigid protocol of a coronation had come right at the end of the service, and in the meantime there had been the most spectacular rite of all—the crowning. In St. Edward's Chapel before that glittering climax Victoria had discarded her crimson robe and had put on a dazzling garment known as the Supertunica of Cloth of Gold. She had also taken off her tiara of diamonds so that she could go bareheaded to the coronation chair.

Without mishap the Archbishop placed the crown on her head, while trumpeters sounded a fanfare and the crashing of drums echoed through the Abbey. Simultaneously, with repeated cries of "Long live Queen Victoria!" the peers and peeresses put on their own coronets.

"A most beautiful and impressive moment" was the phrase later used by Victoria herself to describe that crowning glory. There she sat, a girl of nineteen, slim and small, almost fragile looking, arrayed in the full panoply of her high position, unique in all the world, while around her the leaders of the realm enthusiastically acclaimed their "undoubted Queen."

Quite a number of them were in tears, overcome by the solemnity of that historic moment. The Queen was calm but tense, conscious of the weight of the crown—in every sense of that phrase. In the royal box above the floor of the chancel her mother openly wept tears of joy. Lord Melbourne, standing near Victoria as he held aloft the Sword of State, was also in tears.

One of the few persons with dry eyes was Baroness Lehzen, who had a front seat in a special gallery above the royal box. For her it was an occasion for pride more than tears—the proudest moment of her life. The Queen caught her eye for a fleeting second, and the Baroness gently smiled on her with a loving look. Victoria smiled back.

The crowning was followed by the homage of the peers, who in order of precedence ascended the steps of the dais to touch the crown, kneel before her, and kiss her hand. Their oath of fidelity, which each of them in turn solemnly swore, recalled the distant age of chivalry and the legendary days of King Arthur and his knights:

I do become your liege man of life and limb and of earthly worship, and faith and truth I will bear unto you, to live and die, against all manner of folks, so help me God.

One of the most aged of the peers—certainly he was the most feeble physically—was Lord Rolle, eighty-two years old, who stumbled and fell onto the Abbey floor as he tried to mount the steps leading to the dais. In obvious pain, while the shocked congregation watched in breathless anxiety, he slowly disentangled himself from his robe, which had become wrapped round his legs, and he tremblingly tried to go up the steps once more.

"May I not get up to meet him?" whispered Victoria to Archbishop Howley as she sat in her Chair of Homage. Always inclined to be slow in mental reaction, the bewildered Primate was incapable of prompt response to an emergency. While he seemed to be mumbling to himself, the Queen decided to act.

In her tunic of cloth of gold, and with the diamond-studded crown blazing on her head, she advanced across the platform and walked down three of the five steps to save Lord Rolle the embarrassing effort of trying to ascend again, and in that position, while standing on the steps, she received his homage as he knelt before her and wheezingly repeated the words of the oath of fidelity.

Her thoughtful action, which was deliberately done in breach of strict ceremonial, earned the admiration of everyone present. The cheers as she left the Abbey, when at last the whole service was over, were full of affection as well as enthusiasm. As she passed in procession down the nave she was still wearing the crown. Her right hand held the scepter, and in her left she carried the orb. In place of the crimson robe of state she wore her imperial robe of purple.

Thus attired, she returned in the coach to Buckingham Palace. At every point along the processional route she was vociferously acclaimed. Her diary that night included a glowing, if slightly ungrammatical, description of the gratifying behavior of the crowds. She wrote:

Their good humor and excessive loyalty was beyond everything, and I really cannot say how proud I feel to be the Queen of such a nation. The enthusiasm, affection and loyalty was really touching, and I shall ever remember this day as the *proudest* of my life.

The Queen's coach did not reach Buckingham Palace until six o'clock in the evening, eight hours after it had set out. Despite the long day of continuous strain, Victoria was "really not feeling tired," as she said in her diary; but some of the spectators along the route on the triumphant return journey had commented on her paleness, and at least one very observant man in the crowd, the historian Thomas

69

Carlyle, thought he detected that she was trembling under the weight of the crown.

"God bless you!" he had cried as she passed. With characteristic extravagance of language already familiar to the reading public, he made this pitying comment: "Poor little Queen! She is at an age at which a girl can hardly be trusted to choose a bonnet for herself; yet a task is laid upon her from which an archangel might shrink."

Not for the first time—nor the last, for that matter, since in 1838 he was only at the beginning of a great literary career noteworthy for occasional gross errors of judgment as well as for sustained brilliance of style—Carlyle was very much mistaken in assuming that the Queen was inwardly shrinking from the prospect of the heavy burden to which that day she had sworn fidelity for the rest of her life.

The reality was quite the reverse of his assumption. Victoria really welcomed the great destiny that had been thrust upon her; and on that day she felt absolutely certain that she, and she alone, had been divinely chosen for the highest pinnacle of the realm. Over the many years ahead that inner conviction of her singular selection by Providence remained with her to the end.

Back at the palace at last, she took off her finery and put on an apron. As a relaxing contrast to all the glittering splendors of the long day, she quietly busied herself with the carefree task of giving Dash an evening bath. Although that lively spaniel had originally been her mother's, he gave all his affection to her. She called him "Dashy."

Did she sing as she scrubbed? There is no reliable information on the point, though the dog bath after the coronation is an attested fact of history. The probability was that she did sing; in the happy early years of the reign she was often heard singing. Thomas Carlyle, gravely shaking his head as he walked home to Chelsea while (unknown to him) the dog-bath was in progress, had been very wide of the mark with his pity for the "poor little Queen."

Everybody commended the admirable way in which she had played her part at the coronation. That was especially true of Lord Melbourne, who at a banquet at the palace that night said, "You did it beautifully." Lehzen, too, was full of praise; but at least one distinguished person, the special envoy sent from Turkey to represent the Sultan, could not understand why such a fuss had been made.

"All this for a girl!" he said to another ambassador. As a strict Moslem, holding the belief that women were too inferior to rule over men, he had been bewildered by the events of the day. He felt that the reign could not last long. His doubts on that point were in fact shared by a large number of people, including some of the Queen's subjects, but their reasons for thinking that Victoria would not long remain on the throne were totally different from his: they believed that the British monarchy itself, whether under a man or a woman, was becoming outdated as a system of government and would soon be supplanted by a republic.

How wrong they were! As we all know today, what really happened in history was that during her record-breaking

71

reign Victoria so much enhanced the prestige of royalty that when at last her work was done she left a vastly improved system of constitutional monarchy as the solid basis, not merely the decorative apex, of the British way of life. In the end, that legacy proved to be her greatest memorial—far more impressive than the ornate monument in white marble which now faces Buckingham Palace.

But in the year 1838 that development, that enduring improvement in the status of the crown after decades of disrepute under some of the more profligate of her immediate predecessors, belonged to the future. Behind the colorful splendors of the coronation lay much public discontent. It was a period of hard times for many of Victoria's poorer subjects; and ominous rumblings and grumblings could occasionally be heard from down below.

Near-starvation stalked the meaner streets of some of the big towns. Crime was increasing, especially robbery with violence. For the poor and downtrodden, life was grim. For the children of the poor, work began almost in infancy—if they were lucky enough to find work. *Oliver Twist*, the book that had brought a horrifying glimpse of the workhouse and the thieves' kitchen to Buckingham Palace, was not all fiction.

That was fully realized by some of the nation's rulers, including the Prime Minister, but he often preferred to forget the grim facts. True to the promise he had given the Queen, he somewhat reluctantly set about the task of reading *Oliver Twist;* and he rapidly found that the book was not to his taste. When Victoria eagerly discussed it with him, on learning that he was at last reading it, he tried to turn her mind away from a subject so sordid.

"It's all about workhouses and coffin makers and pickpockets," he said. "I don't like that low debasing view of mankind. I don't like those things. I wish to avoid them. I don't like them in reality, and therefore I don't wish to see them represented."

Realities were indeed disturbing. Yet they had to be faced, as Lord Melbourne himself realized, and a start in that process of facing facts had already been made. The first Reform Act, adopted despite the opposition of William IV, had been passed into law five years before Victoria ascended the throne. It had timidly dealt with some of the more blatant abuses of the electoral system, but it had done nothing to remedy the general state of the nation, which was in the throes of the climactic phases of the Industrial Revolution.

Britain was fast becoming the acclaimed "workshop of the world," a small yet mighty country easily surpassing all others with her soaring production of manufactured goods for export as well as for home consumption. New opportunities were opening up on all sides; the population was rapidly increasing; big fortunes were being made. But in some trades, particularly wool weaving, the steam-driven machines were causing much human misery among displaced workers whose traditional hand skills were no longer required.

Looking back on it now, from the vantage point of the middle of the twentieth century, that early Victorian onrush into the full blast of the Steam Age may seem slow and feeble; yet to the workers involved, women and little children no less than men, the process was even more revolutionary, and certainly far swifter, than the modern surge forward into the era of automation and atomic power.

And there was this somber difference between then and now: for the discarded, cast-off victims of the machines, there was neither unemployment benefit nor public assistance. There was merely idleness and helplessness. Hunger was widespread.

Furthermore, little provision was made for recreation or amenities capable of distracting mens' minds from the harsh realities of the life led by huge colonies of half-starved, unemployed humanity existing in the slums of the big towns. One example of the general lack of the elementary amenities will serve to illustrate the surrounding darkness: in the whole of industrial Lancashire, including the great cities of Manchester and Liverpool, there was only one public park in 1838.

Great progress in achieving material comforts and better education was being made by the middle classes, but on the lower levels of the nation illiteracy and ignorance flourished side by side with brutality. In the year of Victoria's coronation only about half of her 20,000,000 subjects in the United Kingdom could read and write with any degree of facility.

The newspapers, to say nothing of *Oliver Twist*, meant nothing to them. Thirty-three per cent of the men and forty-nine per cent of the women who were married in church during that year were incapable of signing their names in the marriage register. They made a cross—their "mark," as it was called.

Leaders of the demands for reform came mostly from the middle classes. When their attempts to stir up agitation among working people met with growing success, they were regarded by persons in authority as dangerous demagogues. That was particularly applicable to the Chartists, whose ill-organized campaign came into being in 1838.

Rioting and bloodshed occurred in some towns, especially during the following year, but in the end the movement feebly petered out and nothing was gained at the time. Yet the demands put forward seem commonplace in Britain today, merely because nearly all the objectives of the Chartists have long since been achieved by peaceful means—by successive Acts of Parliament, some of which were passed with the Queen's approval during later years of the Victorian era.

They were called "Chartists" because their six-point program was contained in a document they styled "The People's Charter," adopted at a mass meeting in Birmingham, birthplace of the Industrial Revolution, a few weeks after the coronation. Their demands dealt solely with Parliamentary reform, including the setting up of equal electoral districts and the holding of secret ballots at all general elections, and the Charter made no reference to the underlying economic problems of the nation.

In the light of today the aims of the Chartists seem harmless and praiseworthy, but in the anxious year following Victoria's coronation, when rioting took place and men were killed, the widespread campaign was implacably resisted as a major threat to the safety of the state.

The Queen at first regarded the Chartists with a contempt which soon turned to fear, particularly in 1839, when ugly scenes of bloodshed occurred in several cities. At the same time—and in connection with a totally different issue—she herself unwittingly added to public discontent by blundering into a constitutional crisis, in the course of which she obstinately declined to accept the advice of her ministers.

It proved to be her only major mistake of that sort, and it arose over what was fundamentally a minor matter. She soon learned better; she quickly adjusted herself to the spirit of change noticeable everywhere in the land; and years later, regretfully looking back on the causes of the crisis, she freely admitted that she had been in the wrong.

"It was entirely my own foolishness," she said at that later period of realizing her error. But at the time, when the crisis was at its peak, she felt sure she was in the right. Still in her teens—though the incident occurred within a fortnight of her twentieth birthday—she was impetuously determined to get her own way; in consequence she became momentarily unpopular with those of her subjects (quite a large number) who supported the Tories against the Whigs.

Superficially it was a trivial matter, but basically it involved to some extent an important principle that since then —thanks in large measure to Victoria herself—has become an accepted part of the unwritten British constitution: the principle that the monarch should ultimately accept, however reluctantly on occasions, the advice tendered to him or her by ministers responsible to Parliament.

The crisis was derisively called "The Bedchamber Plot"— an appropriate comic label for a minor incident which was not without ridiculous features on both sides of the argument. To the Queen's dismay, Lord Melbourne had temporarily resigned the premiership on May 7, 1839, because his administration had suffered a near-defeat in the House of Commons; she therefore was compelled to ask Sir Robert Peel, on behalf of the Tories, to form a government. When he tried to change the personnel of some of the honorary attendants in the royal household, particularly the Ladies of the Bedchamber, all of them members of prominent Whig families, she flatly refused to meet his wishes.

"Sir Robert has behaved very ill," she said in a letter to Lord Melbourne. "He has insisted on my giving up my ladies, to which I replied that I would never consent. I never saw a man so frightened." In a further letter, written a few hours later on the same day, she stated that Sir Robert would "cut a sorry figure indeed if he resigns on this."

Despite the basic gravity of the issue—involving, as it did, an important question of constitutional practice—there was an undeniably comic element in that memorable confrontation between the Queen and her "frightened" Prime Minister. After all, she was still only a slim girl of nineteen, barely five feet in height, and he was an extremely tall man of fifty-one—a dignified giant in appearance. Towering high above her, he meekly bowed his head and humbly withdrew from the royal presence after she had curtly refused to approve his proffered list of new Ladies of the Bedchamber belonging to Tory families.

Sir Robert was something of a giant in capacity as well as physique. A long career of distinguished public service already lay behind him—with much more to come. As Home Secretary in an earlier Tory administration, at a time when Victoria was still a baby in the nursery at Kensington, he had been the creator of the Metropolitan Police Force, the members of which were the "Bobbies" or "Peelers"—two nicknames bestowed in his honor by a grateful public.

Was "frightened" the right word for a man like that? Perhaps it was a slight exaggeration on Victoria's part. Nevertheless, Sir Robert was definitely shaken, quite overawed, by the inflexible determination she so haughtily displayed at the first audience she ever granted him alone.

He felt that in the circumstances he could not continue as Prime Minister—an office which on that brief first occasion of his tenure, May 9, 1839, he held for only twenty-four hours. He gave up all further attempts to form a government, and none of the other leading Tories had sufficient influence with the party to hope for any chance of succeeding where he had failed.

Lord Melbourne thereupon took up the reins of office once more. The Whig administration thus recalled to power, after a brief but embarrassing interlude, lasted two years longer, despite its shaky majority in both Houses of Parliament. The Queen was naturally delighted to have Melbourne back so soon. As before, they had many entrancing talks together on a variety of subjects.

One new topic they sometimes discussed was the question of whether she ought to marry soon. Victoria was not at all keen on the idea. She was in no hurry—not yet.

A Queen Proposes

Buckingham Palace and Windsor were not the only places where the question of Victoria's marriage was discussed. As a frequent topic of conversation, a talking point for all the gossips in the land, it was a subject that interested everybody. There was much speculation on it — from various angles.

If and when she did at last make up her mind, who would

be the lucky man? It was a question not merely of whether she ought to get married but also of the identity of the likely husband drawn from a short list of eligible suitors.

Not many young men of royal blood in Europe possessed the necessary qualifications and attractions, but among the few potential consorts Prince Albert was by no means accepted by everybody as being the most likely. Furthermore, the Queen was not at all sure whether she really wanted him, despite King Leopold's undisguised and reiterated enthusiasm for an alliance that would obviously strengthen his own growing influence among the crowned dynasties of the Continent.

Victoria sincerely admired her uncle, in whose wisdom she had every reason for reposing confidence, but she did not always accept his advice. On a matter so personally intimate to her, as well as so publicly important to the nation, she naturally turned to Lord Melbourne. In her eyes he seemed more than ever to be not merely Prime Minister but also a venerated parent or guardian.

Melbourne had doubts about all the potential suitors occasionally mentioned by name, and he advised the young Queen to be in no hurry to make up her mind. It was an attitude she fully shared—until she met Albert for a second time.

Three likely candidates for her hand were already being mentioned in the recurring gossip of the day: Her cousin, Prince George of Cambridge; Prince Henry of Orange, younger son of the ruler of Holland; and Prince Albert.

At various times at state balls she had danced with each of them, particularly Prince George, who was just two months older than she was. She certainly liked him, especially as an elegant partner in a quadrille, but despite all the talk she never seriously thought of marrying him. He was destined to succeed to his father's title as Duke of Cambridge and eventually become Commander-in-Chief of the British Army.

As for Prince Henry of Orange—a "timid young man," according to her assessment of him—she was not really in the least bit interested, though such a match had long been suggested; it had been strongly urged in private by the late King in the last year of his life. Behind the scenes, unknown to Victoria at that time, William IV had eagerly mentioned the matter to Lord Melbourne on her seventeenth birthday, but the Prime Minister had then told him that he did not think such a marriage was politically desirable because he felt sure the country would dislike a new dynastic connection with Holland.

Victoria often had Albert in mind, but she had not seen him for two years, and she was secretly half afraid that a second meeting might prove to be disappointing, if not altogether disillusioning. Nevertheless, she still treasured a letter he had sent her when she ascended the throne. That congratulatory message had been in heartfelt terms, far from formal, and had indicated that he fully appreciated the heaviness of her task; but the only mention of love had been general, not particular, as the discreet wording showed:

Now you are Queen of the mightiest land of Europe. In your hand lies the happiness of millions. May Heaven assist you and strengthen you in that high but difficult task! I hope that your reign may be long, happy and glorious, and that your efforts may be rewarded by the thankfulness and love of your subjects.

The first of a number of highly confidential discussions between the Queen and her Prime Minister on the question of marriage took place in the spring of 1839. Together they enumerated various eligible princes in addition to Albert, not one of whom "would do"—as she firmly said. She added: "At present my feeling is quite against ever marrying."

"It's a very great change in the situation," said Melbourne. "It's a very serious thing, both as it concerns the political effect and your own happiness."

"Why need I marry at all for three or four years?" she asked. "It is ten to one I shouldn't agree with anybody. I am so accustomed to having my own way."

"Oh, but you would have it still," retorted the smiling Prime Minister, whose almost daily contacts with her in the preceding two years had taught him, from direct experience, that one of her leading characteristics was an inflexible determination to get her own way.

The real trouble with Victoria at that stage was that her mind was not made up about Albert. Beneath her outward gaiety, and despite her semi-serious talk of never marrying at all, she was secretly bewildered. She knew she liked him. But did she really love him? Melbourne could sense that the problem was worrying her, and he became increasingly concerned about her repeated statement that if possible it was her wish not to marry anybody.

"I don't know about *that*," he said. He himself was becoming worried; therefore he gladly expressed approval when at last she decided to invite Albert and his elder brother Ernest to pay an autumn visit to Windsor. Her chief fear was that if at that second meeting she found that her liking for Albert was not really love—a possible discovery that she felt must entail a firm decision against marriage as an inevitable consequence—then she might be blamed, particularly by King Leopold, for breaking an implied promise of giving him her hand one day.

Subterfuge or deceit of any sort was always unthinkable to Victoria. It had been so when she was a girl—as Baroness Lehzen had noticed and praised—and it remained true of her throughout life. Having decided to invite her Coburg cousins to Windsor, she at once wrote to Uncle Leopold a long letter, sent to Brussels by special courier, explaining exactly how she felt in the matter. One passage stated:

Though all reports of Albert are most favorable, and though I have little doubt I shall like him, still one can never answer beforehand for *feelings*, and I may not have the feeling for him which is requisite to ensure happiness. I may like him as a friend, and as a cousin, and as a *brother*, but not *more*.

Should this be the case (which is not likely), I am very anxious that it should be understood that I am *not* guilty of any breach of promise, for *I never gave any.* I am sure you will understand my anxiety, for I should otherwise, were this not completely understood, be in a very painful position. As it is, I am rather nervous about the visit, for the subject I allude to is not an agreeable one to me.

She was secretly afraid as well as nervous. The reality proved that her fears were groundless. All her worries went in a flash. From the moment she saw Albert again she knew that she was in love—utterly and completely.

In the candid letter to her uncle she had said that in any event there could be no question of marriage for at least "two or three years," but the presence of Albert caused her to make a swift change of mind. No date could then be early enough for her—or for him. They were both genuinely in love.

The fateful meeting took place on October 10, 1839. Traveling overnight in a small steamship, Albert and his brother had a stormy crossing of the North Sea from Antwerp to Tower Pier in London, where they found one of the Queen's equerries waiting with two carriages for the drive to Windsor. Inside the castle, Victoria nervously awaited them on top of the grand staircase. As soon as she saw him the effect on her heart was immediate; at that moment she knew for certain that her fears and worries were at an end.

"It was with some emotion that I beheld Albert, who is *beautiful*," she wrote in her diary. "So handsome and pleasing" was another phrase she used in the privacy of that journal. For her the succeeding few days "passed like a dream," as she said in a letter to King Leopold. By October 15, all was settled—and she did the proposing, as will be seen in a moment. She at once wrote to her uncle:

My mind is quite made up, and I told Albert this morning of it. The warm affection he showed me on learning this gave me great pleasure. He seems *perfection*, and I think I have the prospect of very great happiness before me. I love him more than I can say, and I shall do everything in my power to render the sacrifice he has made (for a *sacrifice* in my opinion it is) as small as I can. . . . I am so much bewildered by it all that I know hardly how to write; but I *do* feel *very, very* happy.

It was not Leap Year; but in her position of reigning Queen the formal proposal of marriage had to come from her—"a nervous thing to do," as she later told one of her aunts, to whom she also said: "Albert would never have presumed to take such a liberty as to propose to the Queen of England."

For his part, he fully realized the position, and he was genuinely overjoyed to accept. Her private version, entered in detail in her diary, explained how she sent for him that morning while she was alone in her room. And then . . .

After a few minutes I said to him that I thought he must be aware that it would make me *too happy* if he would consent to what I wished—to marry me. We embraced each other and he was *so* kind, so affectionate. I told him I was quite unworthy of him. He said he would be very happy, and was so kind, and seemed so happy, that I really felt it was the happiest, brightest moment in my life . . . I feel the happiest of human beings.

For Albert it was "the most joyful possible news," as he wrote next day to Baron Stockmar, who was temporarily in Coburg. In his letter to the delighted baron he also said:

Yesterday, in a private audience, V. declared her love for me, and offered me her hand, which I seized in both mine and pressed tenderly to my lips. She is so good and kind to me that I can scarcely believe such affection should be mine. I know you take part in all my happiness, and so I can pour out my heart to you.

The engagement was secret to begin with: not even Victoria's mother knew of it at the outset. Mainly on the recommendation of Lord Melbourne, who made careful research into old state papers relating to the practices adopted at previous betrothals of reigning sovereigns, the Queen decided to delay any public announcement for several weeks—till a Privy Council had been summoned and Parliament had reassembled after the autumn recess. Melbourne also advised a short engagement, with marriage in the early part of the New Year.

Albert's stay at Windsor was extended to a whole month. He and Victoria exchanged rings; they saw each other every day; they often danced together or sang duets at the piano; they fell deeper and deeper in love; and they were both dismayed when at last the time came for them to part—he to Coburg and she to Buckingham Palace to prepare for the formalities of the official announcement of the betrothal.

"I cannot bear to part from him, for we spend such happy, delightful hours together," she said in another rapturous letter to Uncle Leopold, who had sent his blessings as soon as she told him the news.

The official announcement, read by the Queen in person to a special meeting of the Privy Council, took place in the Throne Room at Buckingham Palace on November 23. She was wearing the ring given to her by Albert, and on her wrist was a bracelet containing a miniature portrait of him. Her hands were trembling so much that she had difficulty in reading the formal declaration, written by Lord Melbourne, of her intention to marry.

Despite the calm self-assurance she generally displayed when occasions of state required a public speech from her, Victoria was sometimes highly nervous inwardly. For example, she had been "dreadfully nervous" (as she afterward confessed to Lord Melbourne) when for the first time she had prorogued Parliament while wearing the Imperial Crown soon after the coronation of the preceding year. To her the Privy Council meeting proved to be "an awful moment."

The marriage was to take place less than three months after that public announcement—on February 10, 1840—and the Queen decided that in a matter affecting her so much personally she preferred the family intimacy of the Chapel Royal at St. James's Palace to the public splendors of Westminster Abbey. Albert heartily agreed with that arrangement; he always disliked excessive display in either dress or ceremony.

During the short interim they wrote to each other daily. On each side those love letters were written partly in English and partly in German, with a preference for German in the more affectionate passages.

To some extent, her letters had to be businesslike as well as affectionate; they had to include numerous references to political matters, especially problems dealing with Albert's future status as Consort. One delicate issue that had to be settled in advance was the question of whether he should be made a peer of the realm. That idea was strongly favored by King Leopold, but she decided against it—on the advice of her ministers.

Such formal and rather mundane topics, mixed up with expressions of love, were unavoidable in the circumstances, but she nevertheless keenly regretted the necessity of having to refer to them. Having explained in one of her longer letters the various public questions she had dealt with on that particular day, she wrote an apology:

I am plaguing you already with tiresome politics, but you will in that find a proof of my love, because I must share with you everything that rejoices me, everything that vexes or grieves me, and I am certain you will take your part in it.

Her daily messages were filled with affection—so much so that if they were to be judged by modern standards they would probably be sneered at as being too gushing. But fashions change, even in love letters. Rapturous phrases were the fashion of the period, and in using them Victoria was not adopting a pose. There was never the slightest trace of falseness in anything she wrote; she really meant what she said.

It was the same with Albert, who frequently began his letters with "Dear, splendid Victoria," or "Dearest, deeply loved Victoria." On one occasion he wrote: "Even in my dreams I never imagined that I should find so much love on earth."

People near to the Queen, especially Lord Melbourne, could see that she was genuinely in love. As leader of the official opposition in the House of Commons, Sir Robert Peel occasionally saw her at state functions, and in that one matter, at least, he fully shared the Prime Minister's opinion.

"She is as full of love as Juliet," said Sir Robert to a friend as the date of the marriage drew near.

Prince Albert arrived in England two days before the wedding. For him the move from Coburg meant a new life in every respect: it entailed not only matrimony but also a permanent change of nationality. Victoria had made special arrangements for him to be naturalized as a British subject before the marriage.

Welcoming crowds saw him land at Dover on the morning of February 8, 1840, accompanied by his father and brother. At Canterbury he interrupted their drive to London in order to attend a service in the cathedral—a gesture of future devotion to the Anglican Church which Lord Melbourne commended as "a very good thing to do."

In London that evening Victoria awaited him at the main entrance to Buckingham Palace, facing the center gates. She proudly noted that he was "looking beautiful and so well." They embraced, and she led him by the hand into his new home.

At a private ceremony held in Buckingham Palace next day, which was a Sunday, the oaths of naturalization as a British subject were administered to Albert by the Lord Chancellor, acting in his capacity of head of the judicature and legal system. That evening the prospective bride and bridegroom read the marriage service together to ensure that they would not falter over any words at the actual ceremony.

On Monday immense crowds cheered the Queen as she drove to the Chapel Royal. Her shimmering gown of white satin had a deep flounce of Honiton lace, and she was wearing a diamond necklace with diamond earrings and a large sapphire brooch presented to her by Albert.

She carried a nosegay of orange flowers given to her by her mother, who accompanied her in the carriage, and at the ceremony she was attended by twelve young trainbearers dressed in white and carrying bouquets of white roses. To each of them the Queen later presented a turquoise brooch as a memento of the historic day.

The elder of Victoria's two surviving royal uncles, the Duke of Sussex, gave her away, and the service was conducted by the Archbishop of Canterbury. Happily, on that occasion it was the duty of Albert, not the Archbishop, to see that there was no painful error in the ceremony of the ring. He made no mistake in that or in any other part of the service.

"I felt so happy when the ring was put on—and by Albert," wrote the Queen, whose diary description of the scene, detailed and vivid, included a passage applicable to all church marriages:

> The ceremony was very imposing and fine and simple, and I think ought to make an everlasting impression on everyone who promises at the Altar to *keep* what he or she promises.

She and her husband had a tumultuous reception from the crowds during their short drive from St. James's to Buckingham Palace. Their healths were enthusiastically drunk at the wedding breakfast—which, despite the name, was really a glittering banquet held at lunchtime in the main dining room. The cake, monumental in shape and size, weighed 300 pounds. Icing cupids were wreathed round the base, and the summit consisted of a figure of Britannia giving her blessing to the royal newlyweds, who were represented by figures dressed in the white robes of ancient Romans.

A brief honeymoon was spent at Windsor Castle. There

was no prouder man than Lord Melbourne among the group of distinguished guests who smilingly waved them on their journey as they drove through the gates of Buckingham Palace. He felt that his great task of ensuring an auspicious opening for Victoria's reign had at last been accomplished, and he was happy to think that henceforth the Queen would have the valuable advice, as well as the constant companionship, of a husband in whom he already had the utmost confidence. Thereafter he was quite content to play a secondary role in her life.

"Nothing could have gone off better," he told her before the departure for Windsor. His eyes filled with tears as he kissed her hand and said, "God bless you, Ma'am."

She knew he felt that the future would bring complete success, and she recalled that on an earlier occasion when she had discussed with him the question of marriage he had said: "You will be very much more comfortable. A woman cannot stand alone for any time, in whatever position she may be."

Albert's future title and status in the realm were matters of deep concern to the Queen, who thought that in the order of precedence he ought to be officially ranked equal with herself—an idea that was strongly opposed by a powerful group in Parliament, especially some peers of ancient lineage. They were jealous of allowing too much to him, either in title or money.

"Prince Consort" was the most she could ever bestow on him; and in fact it was not until as late as 1857 that that title was conferred by her personally under the device of Royal Letters Patent, a method that did not depend on the will of Parliament but was solely her own prerogative. In the meantime he was known as Prince Albert.

"He ought to be, and is, above me in everything really," she wrote. In the early years her love was such that she would have been quite willing to take second place nominally, but she knew that that was impossible, and she therefore said, "I wish that he should be equal in rank with me." Parliament thought otherwise, both at the time of the marriage and at all times thereafter. It was a source of continuing grievance to the Queen, who always felt that her husband's abilities were not sufficiently recognized.

Victoria was further offended by Parliament's decision, taken against the wishes of Lord Melbourne, to reduce Albert's proposed allowance from £50,000 to £30,000 a year. Opposition to the larger sum had come from a temporary alliance in the House of Commons between Tories and Radicals, who by acting together, in strange and unusual partnership, were able to defeat Melbourne's original proposal by 104 votes.

Despite those public rebuffs on the threshold of the Queen's married life—caused mainly by aggrieved Tories who bitterly remembered and resented her rigid attitude at the time of the Bedchamber Plot—the union with Albert proved to be a complete success, as Uncle Leopold had forecast. It was a happy marriage in every way.

Domestically Victoria's life was one of utter contentment,

and politically the advice of her husband was almost invariably wise and farsighted. It was due to him more than to any other single influence that better relations were slowly but surely established between the monarchy and the Tories, particularly Sir Robert Peel.

With a foresight that the Queen did not at first share, Albert could see that sooner or later the main opposition party would one day be called upon to form the government, and he began to cultivate better relations with some of the Tory leaders, especially Peel, for whose outstanding abilities he soon developed sincere respect. In his turn, Peel greatly admired Albert's qualities. They became personal friends.

Largely because of her husband's reiterated praise, Victoria also began to realize that Sir Robert was a man of the highest integrity. But Lord Melbourne still held—and always would hold—top place in her esteem as the best as well as the first Prime Minister of her long reign.

During the early months of the marriage the Whig government continued in office, though often in danger of defeat. Lord Melbourne's physical powers were obviously waning; he was losing force and grip. Nevertheless, some progressive measures were enacted, and the most memorable event of the period, welcomed by all shades of opinion in Parliament, was the introduction of a system of universal penny postage with adhesive stamps. In adopting that idea Britain easily led the world.

Hitherto postal charges had varied according to distance, wherever addressed, and had been collected on delivery

Some of the rates were absurdly high. For instance, the cost of sending a letter consisting of only one sheet from London to Edinburgh had been one shilling, three and a half pence—equivalent to at least six shillings, or about eighty-five cents, in terms of present money values. Mr. Rowland Hill, a schoolmaster and mathematician who had made a study of the problem and was eventually rewarded with a knighthood, showed by means of his careful calculations that a flat rate of one penny, paid by the sender irrespective of distance, would be profitable in the long term, and after much discussion Parliament adopted his scheme.

The first adhesive stamps—highly treasured today by philatelists, to whom they are "Penny Blacks"—were issued in May of 1840. They bore a portrait of the young Queen's head in profile, and she herself was delighted by the new idea. The portrait was a graceful and accurate engraving, skillfully executed and easily identifiable.

Until then, few of the Queen's subjects had known what she really looked liked. Photographs were rudimentary—Fox Talbot, another of the great Victorian pioneers, was still engaged in only primitive experiments in 1840—and pictures in newspapers, to say nothing of glossy magazines, did not exist. Now everybody in the land could see what the Queen looked like; they could buy her portrait for a penny.

That simple link between the crown and the people was the beginning of an utterly new public attitude toward the British monarchy. As an institution it became less remote and it soon gained widespread popularity. That process applied particularly to the middle classes, with whom the Queen and her husband became more and more associated as the years advanced and their children were born. Their quiet family life, impeccably respectable, was in marked contrast to the profligate ways of several recent predecessors at Windsor.

At the outset nothing contributed more to that changed relationship, that sense of becoming closely identified with the monarchy, than the issue of the penny postage stamps. Over the centuries hitherto, the ruler had seemed aloofly remote from the ordinary people. Kings or queens of the past had been known to only a relatively few privileged persons revolving in the narrow limits of the court circle. By contrast, the new stamps seemed to bring Victoria into every home.

Still showing the girlish profile, the original picture of the Queen was destined to remain on United Kingdom stamps even after Victoria had reached middle age. At first the Penny Blacks were printed on sheets of paper that had to be cut with scissors—perforations were not introduced till 1854—but from the start they were adhesive. That apparently elementary device of gum on the back was in itself an admired novelty of the early period; it seemed to be a symbol of the general progress noticeable in many aspects of everyday life.

Postage stamps spread throughout the world, though not immediately. Brazil, the first country to follow the British example, adopted the idea in 1843. In the United States local stamps of limited range were already in existence in several cities, but the first general issue was not begun till 1847, and the French did not follow suit till 1849, nearly a decade after Britain had shown the way.

The increasing popularity of the Queen received further stimulus from an unexpected and dark quarter—from the pistol of a would-be assassin. A wave of sympathy swept the country when two shots were fired at her while she was driving with Albert along Constitution Hill on June 10, 1840.

It was the first of seven attempts on her life during the reign, with the last not due till 1882. In nearly every case—and this first one was clearly in that category—the assailant was a lunatic. The attempts were no less dangerous for that.

On Constitution Hill the frenzied attacker, a youth of eighteen named Edward Oxford, was immediately captured, and at his trial he was found to be insane. Though fired from a distance of only five yards, the two shots missed. Despite the narrowness of the escape, Victoria and her husband displayed not the slightest trace of fear. They continued on their drive, to show the people that they were safe. Their brave conduct in the sudden emergency, as unexpected as it was horrifying, was greatly admired.

Shocked expressions of sympathy, combined with congratulations on the escape, poured in from all quarters. King Leopold wrote of the "horror" he felt on hearing the news, and he added: "That you have shown great fortitude is not to be doubted, and it will make a great and good impression."

Not one of the assailants at various times thereafter came

101

near to success. Some of them seemed to be almost half-hearted as well as half-crazed. Yet it became a curious fact of history that more assassination attempts were made on Victoria, blameless in every way, than on any other monarch during the centuries preceding her.

In face of such dastardly attacks, so utterly undeserved, the Queen invariably showed imperturbable bravery; she was always the calmest person present on each of those horrifying occasions. Her popularity with the vast majority of her subjects continued to increase. At first—and with the exception of the solid middle classes, who greatly admired him—Albert did not fully share in that rising tide of public favor.

Perhaps that was mainly because he was still to some extent regarded as "a foreigner," a member of a lower species in most British eyes of those days. But persons within the court circle, including leaders of the opposition as well as ministers, quickly realized that his influence was wholly in the best interests of the national welfare.

Behind the scenes he was beginning to act almost in the role of the Queen's private secretary when dealing with affairs of state. His tactful advice, always well considered, provided constant comfort and support to her. At the Queen's first public appearance before Parliament after the marriage —it was on the occasion of proroguing Parliament on August 11, 1840—he was given an armchair beside the throne on the dais in the House of Lords.

She was no longer alone on such occasions, which hitherto

she had dreaded as nervous ordeals. She felt great reassurance, with a happy sense of new-found confidence, in having him so close beside her.

Another source of immense satisfaction to her—particularly in view of Parliament's earlier reluctance to grant Albert the rank she felt he deserved—was the decision, readily approved by both Houses, to nominate him as potential Regent when it was known that she was going to have a baby.

That formal step of naming a Regent—and happily it was indeed purely formal, seeing that it was never required—was an inescapable part of constitutional practice. Had the Queen died in childbirth, with the baby surviving, a Regency would have been necessary until the child's coming-of-age. There were no complications, however, and on November 21, 1840, Victoria had her first child, a daughter.

"It will be a boy next time," she said, in a confident prediction that came true in the following year. The baby girl was named Victoria Adelaide Marie Louise. Her public title was Princess Royal, but in the privacy of the family she was generally called "Vicky," sometimes "Pussy."

She proved to be a healthy baby. Soon she became a very bright child, vigorous and full of fun. As part of the fun when she began to talk ,he sometimes expressed pouting resentment at her nickname.

"I'm not Pussy! I'm the Princess Royal!" she then exclaimed, stamping her feet in disgust. But that was some years ahead, when the family had grown and she had several brothers and sisters.

Marriage and motherhood suited Victoria. For two decades, from 1840 to 1860, she was rarely unhappy. They proved to be the best years of her life, when no portent of later sorrows clouded her serene horizon.

"It will be a boy next time," she had said. She was quite right. At Buckingham Palace on November 9, 1841, her heir was born: Albert Edward, Duke of Cornwall, soon to be officially created Prince of Wales, and later—much later, in far-off 1901, when he was nearly sixty years old—destined to ascend the throne as Edward VII.

On the announcement of the birth there was great rejoicing throughout the land. This was the first male heir to be born to a reigning sovereign for seventy-nine years. The previous occasion had been in 1762, early in the reign of George III, when the baby who eventually became Prince Regent and then George IV was born at St. James's Palace.

Of the two names chosen at the christening ceremony a few months later, "Albert" was of course after his own father and "Edward" was in honor of the Queen's father, the late Duke of Kent. To the outer world he was Prince Edward, but in the family he was always "Bertie."

"I hope and pray that he may be like his dearest Papa," said the Queen in a letter to King Leopold. No doubt smiling as she wrote, she also said that "Pussy is *not* at all pleased with her brother." In all, Victoria was destined to have nine children, each of whom grew to healthy maturity at a period when in general the infantile mortality rate was alarmingly high; but three of them died as adults in the course of her own long lifetime.

Let us look ahead for a moment to get a brief picture of each of the royal children, in the order of their birth:

1840, Victoria, Princess Royal, married in 1858 Frederick William, Prince of Prussia, who for a brief reign was

Emperor Frederick I of Germany. Their eldest son became Wilhelm II, the Kaiser of the First World War. She died in 1901 after unhappy and neglected years of widowhood.

1841, Albert Edward, Prince of Wales, later King Edward VII, married in 1863 Princess Alexandra of Denmark. He died in 1910, and his second son became George V.

1843, Princess Alice, married in 1862 the Grand Duke of Hesse. She died in 1878.

1844, Prince Alfred, Duke of Edinburgh and of Saxe-Coburg-Gotha, married in 1874 the Grand Duchess Marie Alexandrovna of Russia. He died in 1900.

1846, Princess Helena, married in 1866 Prince Christian of Schleswig-Holstein, and died in 1923.

1848, Princess Louise, married in 1871 the Duke of Argyle, and died in 1939.

1850, Prince Arthur, Duke of Connaught, married in 1879 Princess Louisa of Prussia. He lived until 1942.

1853, Prince Leopold, Duke of Albany, married in 1882 Princess Helena of Weldeck-Pyrmont (Germany), and died 1884.

1857, Princess Beatrice, married in 1885 Prince Henry of Battenberg, and died in 1944.

All the children were strictly brought up, especially the Prince of Wales, who was given an education that by modern standards would be regarded as over-sheltered and far too intensive. One change made in the arrangements of the royal household during the early 1840's was that Baroness Lehzen went back to Germany to live in retirement. The walls of her home there were covered with portraits of the Queen, from whom she received a gushing letter every week.

Baron Stockmar continued as private adviser, though his influence lessened as fundamental changes took place in the conduct of public affairs at the highest level, with more and more power being wielded by the Cabinet as the years advanced. One of the greatest of those political transformations was that after a general election in 1841 Sir Robert Peel became Prime Minister—an enforced appointment which the Queen at first disliked but later came to welcome, even describing Sir Robert as "a kind and true friend."

It was a period of bad trade, due to a temporary slump, together with harsh conditions of employment. Slowly but surely improvements were made, and outstanding among the reformers in the new Parliament was Lord Ashley, soon to succeed his father as Earl of Shaftesbury. He was tireless—and eventually successful—in advocating improvement in conditions of employment.

Side by side with demands for betterment in the conditions of the people, enormous developments were taking place in science and industry. New machines were being introduced every year, and the swift growth of railways, spreading to all corners of the land, encouraged spectacular achievements in engineering, particularly bridge building and tunneling.

The Queen's first experience of railway travel occurred on June 13, 1842. The trip was from Windsor to Paddington station in London, a distance of only twenty-one miles but a journey that was epoch-making in the circumstances, since it at last convinced everybody that the new form of locomotion must be safe, for the Queen herself consented to use it.

On several occasions when traveling to or from Windsor Prince Albert had patronized the new line, and it was mainly because of his persuasions that Victoria agreed to try it. Albert had been an early convert to the new form of transport, though sometimes he had been heard to say half-humorously to the guard on alighting at Windsor, "Not quite so fast next time, Mr. Conductor, if you please."

The Queen was so delighted with the experience that on every occasion thereafter, whenever she visited various parts of the kingdom, she went by rail. In a letter to Uncle Leopold she said, "I am quite charmed with it."

Telegraphy was another British invention making headway at this time. It was of special value to the railway companies, who were foremost in using it, and in 1846 the Electric Telegraph Company was formed to exploit it for public service. In that same year the world's first submarine cable was laid—a small yet decisive step forward in the quickening march of progress, consisting of no more than a half-mile length of cable linking the opposite shores of Portsmouth harbor.

The first international cable, laid across the seabed from Dover to Calais, came in 1850. It worked perfectly for a few months, until a French fisherman unwittingly hauled up a length of it and at once imagined that he had caught a sea serpent of length so enormous that he could not hope to land it whole. He cut off a slice to take home as a specimen of his remarkable catch. A completely new cable, better protected than its unlucky predecessor, had to be laid.

Not only in science but also in the arts, particularly literature, great developments were taking place in the middle phase of the Victorian epoch. While the first cable was being laid between Britain and France, Alfred Tennyson, then forty years old, was made Poet Laureate in succession to Wordsworth, and his *In Memoriam,* the most moving of his major works, was published.

Dickens was at his zenith, producing book after book in apparently effortless succession. Yet he was by no means alone as a front-rank novelist destined to achieve shining immortality; the Victorian literary firmament contained a whole galaxy of first-magnitude stars.

Some ideas of the simultaneous dazzle in that crowded sky may be obtained by taking only one year as an example.

In 1847 the following novels were published for the first time: *Dombey and Son* (Dickens), *Wuthering Heights*

(Emily Brontë), *Jane Eyre* (Charlotte Brontë), *Vanity Fair* (Thackeray).

Hardly in the same class, but noteworthy because of its author's growing importance in public affairs, *Tancred*, a political-social novel by Benjamin Disraeli, appeared in the bookshops for the first time in that same year. Another prominent politician of the period, Lord Macaulay, also was earning literary immortality, though in a different field from that of the novelists: by that year he had completed the first two volumes of his *History of England*, a monumental work distinguished alike for breadth of learning and magnificence of style. Charles Darwin, newly moved to his home at Downe, in Kent—today kept as a public memorial to him—was quietly assembling the material for a book of revolutionary impact, *The Origin of Species.*

Science and literature were the two greatest spheres of Victorian achievement. Mental boundaries were being pushed back everywhere, to disclose new horizons undreamed of in preceding centuries; and at the same time the frontiers of the British Empire were being swiftly expanded. One of those imperial acquisitions brought a remarkable addition to the crown, in a double sense.

Because trouble had broken out in northwest India, entailing a military expedition, the province of the Punjab was incorporated in the Empire. As token of submission, the Maharajah presented to the Queen the enormous diamond known as the Koh-i-noor, meaning "Mountain of Light." After being specially cut, it was fitted into one of the crowns.

Another acquisition by the Queen came from an unexpected quarter, previously unknown by her. In this instance the gift was quite personal, as distinct from any question of its being for the state. On the death of an eccentric miser named John Camden Neild, whose father had been silversmith to George IV, it was found that his will bequeathed the whole of his fortune, amounting to £500,000, to the Queen personally.

The large sum thus unexpectedly obtained was carefully invested, and it helped to swell the riches she was gradually accumulating for her growing family. In making her investments she received shrewd advice from Prince Albert—always farsighted in money matters, as in most things. On the whole, their private mode of life was never extravagant, though inevitably on occasions the Queen had to spend considerable amounts on public functions.

The phase of slump had been succeeded by boom, with expanding overseas trade and increasing prosperity at home, and in consequence, people with money often displayed extravagance—especially if their money happened to be newly acquired. Dress and food were the two main outlets for ostentatious expenditure. The crinoline was in fashion, and banquets in those days included a vast choice of courses.

The royal family naturally followed the fashion whenever they entertained at Buckingham Palace. One of the printed menus for such an occasion, headed "Her Majesty's Dinner," has been preserved. As a sample of mid-Victorian banquets, solid as well as ornate, it deserves to be set out in full:

Soups

Clear soup with Quenels   Cream of Ptarmigan

Cream of Lettuce

—

Fish

Braised stuffed Pike   Eels and tartar sauce

Turbot and lobster sauce

—

Seasoned dishes

Roast best end of Venison   Pigeon pie

—

Entrées

Roast Spring Chicken with cauliflower

Stuffed breast of Lamb   Stewed Chicken with cucumbers

Sausages of Chicken   Braised breast of Veal

Oyster pies

—

Roast

Leverets   Turkeys

Wheatears

—

Spicy Dishes — Appetizers

Waffles   Lemon Pudding

—

Cold Dishes

Slice of Salmon and mayonnaise sauce   Russian salad

Macaroni au gratin   Poached eggs in jelly

Globe artichokes   French bean salad

Cinnamon blancmange   Puffed pastry with apple

Fruit flan   Almond biscuits   Peaches and rice

—

Sideboard

Roast Beef   Roast Mutton

Hashed Venison

Clear soup and rice   Chicken soup

Greengage tart

While their own personal fortune was growing, the royal couple decided to purchase estates in two widely separated parts of the realm they both delighted in visiting: the Isle of Wight and Scotland. A large new house at Osborne, almost on the seashore opposite Cowes, was completed in 1846, and Balmoral, a beautiful estate in the Highlands, covering 25,000 acres, was a later acquisition.

Prince Albert took the closest interest in supervising the plans for the construction of Balmoral Castle, which was largely his own design, and for that reason the Queen always regarded it as her favorite residence. But his greatest achievement in her eyes was the encouragement he gave to the building of the Great Exhibition of 1851, which was held in Hyde Park and came to be known as the Crystal Palace when it was afterward transferred to the London suburb of Sydenham.

Despite much opposition from politicians, who felt that the result would be financial failure, Albert firmly sponsored the project of holding the biggest-ever international exhibition designed to show the products of many lands, with special emphasis on British mechanical ingenuity. From 234 drawings submitted by various architects he personally chose the scheme for a gigantic glasshouse submitted by James Paxton.

The exhibition was a brilliant success. During the six months it was open in Hyde Park 6,000,000 people paid to see it. In the end there was a profit of £186,000, most of which was used for purchasing sites for several famous national museums in Kensington, among them the Victoria and Albert, which received permanent endowment.

Tennyson, the new Poet Laureate, felt impelled to write a poem in honor of the exhibition. It was hardly in his best style, but it expressed the prevailing sentiment:

> She brought a vast design to pass
> When Europe and the scatter'd ends
> Of our fierce world did meet as friends
> And brethren in her halls of glass.

Unhappily the spirit of international brotherhood engendered by the Great Exhibition did not last long. Soon the clouds of approaching war were lowering over Europe. The scene of that ugly storm was the Crimea, a Russian peninsula jutting out into the Black Sea.

It was the first European war of the reign, and in it British troops suffered great privation. It could be described as the first of Victoria's major public sorrows, as distinct from her private griefs still to come.

In the Shadows

The Crimean War, in which Britain, France and Sardinia aided Turkey's resistance to Russian encroachments on the decaying Ottoman Empire, lasted nearly two years. It resulted in the defeat of tsarist designs for expansion, but the victory involved much hardship to British front-line forces, due mainly to bad administration in the higher ranks of the ill-prepared army.

Both the Queen and the Prince Consort ceaselessly prodded the government to make better arrangements for the soldiers. In particular, Victoria was appalled by the high rate of epidemic diseases at base hospitals, mostly cholera, which caused far more casualties than those inflicted by the enemy in the fighting line.

She greatly admired the heroic work of Florence Nightingale, pioneer of the modern military nursing service, whose energetic and sometimes ruthless reforms—accomplished at first with the aid of a devoted group of only thirty-eight trained nurses—eventually reduced from forty-two per cent to two per cent the death rate among admissions to the hospitals.

At the request of the Queen, the Lady with the Lamp, as she was called by the grateful soldiers, drew up a lengthy report—"Notes on the British Army"—which provided the basis of permanent transformations in the Army medical service. Victoria presented her with a gold brooch of special design, consisting of the royal crown and cypher, with the St. George's cross in red enamel, and with this inscription: "Crimea. Blessed Are The Merciful."

In the summer of 1857, with Europe at peace once more, the Queen presented for the first time another sort of decoration, the Victoria Cross. The idea of instituting a new medal for superb bravery, open to all ranks of the armed services, was cordially approved by Victoria, who personally decided that the cross should bear the words, "For Valour" instead of "For The Brave," as had been originally proposed.

It was in that same summer that the Indian Mutiny broke out. That was another source of deep anxiety to the Queen. But her greatest sorrows did not come until 1861, which proved to be the most tragic year of her life. The wounds then inflicted on her mind and heart never healed; she was a changed woman thereafter.

In March her mother died at the age of seventy-four. The Queen had not fully recovered from that private grief when the Prince Consort became ill in the autumn. At first he seemed to be suffering from only a minor complaint, possibly influenza, and not until it was too late did the doctors diagnose typhoid fever.

Although only forty-two years of age, Albert already had the appearance of an old man, with bald head and lined face. The truth was that he had been wearing himself out in incessant devotion to every detail of state affairs. Never robust, he had said to Victoria on one occasion:

"I do not cling to life. You do; but I set no store by it. I am sure that if I had a severe illness I should give up at once. I should not struggle for life."

Those somber words were tragically fulfilled. During a visit to Sandhurst on November 22, 1861, when he had inspected new buildings in the Royal Military College at that Berkshire village, he caught a chill from which he never recovered. For several days after his return to Windsor he insisted on continuing to deal with state papers, until increasing infirmity forced him to give up and take to his bed.

Nearly a fortnight passed before the dreadful truth became apparent. Not until the Saturday morning of December 14 was the first public bulletin issued. It was a grave message for the nation: "His Royal Highness the Prince Consort is in a most critical state."

That was the first indication the outer world received of the gravity of Albert's condition. Only a few hours of life were left to him; he died that night at ten-fifty. At midnight the great bell of St. Paul's Cathedral was tolled as a mournful signal to the stunned people of London.

Victoria was distraught, utterly crushed. Her sorrowful crying could be heard down the corridors of the castle. For hours that was the only sound to come from her; she was quite unable to speak—nor to sleep during that night. She never fully recovered from this cruel blow to her private happiness. Henceforth the story of her life was completely different from anything that had gone before.

It was as if an entirely new reign had begun. With the Queen always dressed in widow's black, the new reign of solitude and solemn mourning was destined to last nearly four decades, during the first few years of which she rarely appeared in public.

On the Sunday, the day after the death, a special edition of the *London Gazette* was issued, with this official announcement:

> On Saturday night, the 14th instant, at ten minutes before 11 o'clock, His Royal Highness the Prince Consort departed this life, at Windsor Castle, to the inexpressible

grief of Her Majesty and all the Royal Family. The death of this illustrious Prince will be deeply mourned by all Her Majesty's faithful and attached subjects as an irreparable loss to Her Majesty, the Royal Family, and the Nation.

In the same issue of the *Gazette* a bulletin signed by four doctors gave a somewhat misleading version of Victoria's condition: "The Queen, although overwhelmed with grief, bears her bereavement with calmness and has not suffered in health." The description "calmness" was not really accurate. It was true that she had not suffered in physical health, but she was suffering gravely from shock; she had received a crushing blow that permanently changed her outlook and mode of life.

To this present day, a hundred years after the sad event, the heartbroken letters she wrote from Windsor to King Leopold are harrowing to read. Some of the shrill lamentations in those tear-stained documents still seem to echo the cries of grief, the anguished sobbing, heard in the castle on that night long ago:

My life as a happy one is *ended!* The world is gone for me! I had hoped with such instinctive certainty that God never *would* part us and would let us grow old together. . . . Too *awful*, too cruel. . . . I know you will help me in my utter darkness. It is but for a short time, and *then* I go—*never, never* to part.

Ten days after the death, by which time Victoria had partially recovered her strength, though still overwhelmed with grief, she wrote to her uncle about her intentions for the future. She explained that the example of Albert, with his constant devotion to duty, would always remain with her; and the promise she then made to King Leopold in the hour of her agony was kept to the end of her life:

> It is my firm resolve, my irrevocable decision, that *his* wishes—*his* plans—about everything, *his* views about everything, are to be *my law*. And no human power will make me swerve from what he decided and wished.

By then she had gone to Osborne for Christmas— an annual custom that she and Albert had observed ever since they built the house. More perceptive than her doctors, she described her condition as "miserably weak and utterly shattered." She shut out of her mind all ideas of Christmas celebrations that year. Her thoughts were fixed on Albert, to the exclusion of all else; and throughout her remaining life—a period in itself almost as long as her late husband's whole life—she did everything possible to keep his memory alive. At Windsor and the other royal residences nothing that recalled him to her was allowed to be disturbed.

"I am on a dreary sad pinnacle of solitary grandeur," said the Queen. During the first few years following the bereavement she never for one moment permitted heself to descend from that lonely and gloomy height. In that bleak period of

aloof sorrow she was hardly ever seen in public—except fleet-
ingly, on her frequent journeys to Osborne or Balmoral—
and she flatly refused, despite the pleadings of her ministers,
to attend such ceremonies as the opening of Parliament.

That was the outward picture—the public picture. Behind
the scenes, bent day after day over her desk in ceaseless
study of state documents, she was tireless in fulfilling her
resolve to continue as Albert would have wished. Even at
the apex of her sorrow—the "dreary sad pinnacle"—she was
ever mindful of her royal duties to the nation.

The outer world did not realize that despite her public
aloofness she was still very much the Queen in private. Mut-
tured grumblings about her continuing seclusion became
audible, and at length they became outspoken. On the third
anniversary of Albert's death *The Times* published a pon-
derous leading article on the subject.

In all bereavements there is a time when the days of
mourning be looked upon as past. The living have their
claims as well as the dead; and what claims can be more
imperative than those of a great nation and the society of
one of the first European capitals? For every reason we
trust that now that three years have elapsed, and every
honour that affection and gratitude could pay to the memory of the Prince Consort has been offered, her Majesty
will think of her subjects' claims and the duties of her high
station, and not postpone them longer to the indulgence
of an unavailing grief.

It was a forthright and sharp reproof, made all the more cruel by the deliberate selection of date for publication. The Queen was deeply hurt. In her own intimate circle she bitterly complained of the unfairness of the rebuke, as she saw it, but she made no attempt at public reply. For several years more her scheduled mode of life remained unchanged.

Fresh pangs were added to her private sorrows when King Leopold died in 1865. For Victoria it meant not only the removal of the last link with the older generation of her royal relatives but also the loss of a beloved father-figure. His demise seemed to accentuate her loneliness.

For many years Leopold had filled a unique position as the central adviser of a wide circle of related rulers enthroned over the diverse peoples of numerous Continental nations. His duties in that respect now largely devolved upon her: she was increasingly regarded as being the supreme head of Europe's crowned heads. In filling that new role she remained true to character: she allowed nothing to escape her alert eye. Few things could happen in the courts of Europe without her consent—or criticism, which was chilling, sometimes icy.

Thus in old age she became the mother-figure of Europe as well as of the Empire. Her correspondence with other monarchs and princes was enormous, almost staggering when considered from the one point of view of the sheer labor involved in the writing process. Nor were her personal letters—always written in her own hand—confined to royalty. It was in that same year of 1865, when King Leopold died, that

President Lincoln was assassinated in Washington. Victoria's horrified first thoughts were naturally for the widow, to whom she wrote:

No one can better appreciate than I can—who am myself *utterly broken-hearted* by the loss of my beloved husband, who was the light of my life, my stay, *my all*—what your suffering must be.

The years passed, and gradually the Queen emerged from complete seclusion, though at no time thereafter did she participate in public duties to the same extent as she had joyously fulfilled when Albert had been at her side. The first faltering sign of the slow change came in February of 1866, when she reluctantly agreed to open Parliament in person.

Five years had gone by since she had last performed that service. She grudgingly assented to the earnest pleadings of her ministers, who emphasized that the opening of Parliament was one of the most essential duties of any reigning monarch, but she said that in no circumstances could she undertake the task of reading the official speech provided for her.

She also declined to wear her robe of state. That was because she felt that widow's black, not a crimson robe, was the only garb appropriate to her bereaved condition. In the Lords' Chamber the robe was placed on a chair beside the throne, where she sat silent in a black silk evening dress while at her command the Lord Chancellor read her speech.

Her part in the proceedings was passive; yet she neverthe-less felt it to be "a dreadful ordeal," as she told her Prime Minister, who by then was Earl Russell, first holder of that title. She returned to Osborne immediately afterward.

A year later she again appeared at a great public cere-mony in London. It was for a purpose that pleased her very much, despite the anguished memories that must have been passing through her mind. As part of a national memorial scheme in honor of the late Consort, the government had decided to build the Royal Albert Hall in Kensington, within sight of the palace where Victoria had been born; she readily agreed to lay the foundation stone, though she found the ordeal almost unnerving.

The stone-laying took place on February 5, 1867. The Queen's voice in replying to an address of welcome was so faint—little more than a whisper—that it was audible to only a handful of distinguished persons standing near her. A vast concourse, with all the men bareheaded and most of the women in black, watched the ceremony, but until they read the newspaper reports they did not know what the Queen had said in expressing her gratitude.

It was not until four years later that the huge building was completed. By that time Victoria was beginning to look al-most happy once more. She was delighted to perform the official opening ceremony; and the watching crowd was equally delighted to observe that she seemed to be not only in excellent health but also in unfeigned and undisguised good spirits. She had a smile for everyone.

She was still in mourning—black silk dress, black gloves, black bonnet, decorated with a few white flowers—but the worst phase of her gloom had evidently gone. Nothing had contributed more to that welcome change than her growing interest in her family circle, which was rapidly expanding and bringing back lively memories of her own childhood.

Her grandchildren were becoming numerous—destined to total forty as the years advanced, with thirty-seven great-grandchildren up to the time of her death—and she always felt happy in their prattling company. It became her custom to present each grandchild with a gold watch on attaining the age of ten. Invariably she accompanied the gift with a personal letter of good wishes from "Ever your loving Grand-mama."

Some of those grandchildren grew to maturity and ascended thrones in various kingdoms or principalities during her own lifetime. Toward the end there were few royal houses in Europe that were not linked to her in some way, either by direct descent or by marriage in the second or third generation.

As old age crept on, she became "The mother of many nations"—a phrase coined by Disraeli, who proved to be by far the most colorful of all the ten Prime Ministers of the long Victorian era. It was during the second of his two periods of office that the reign attained new splendors.

Benjamin Disraeli was the seventh of Victoria's ten Prime Ministers, but in the order of her esteem he ranked as second only to Lord Melbourne, who had died twenty years before Disraeli achieved that highest office. His first premiership in 1868 was limited to ten months, after which defeat at the polls forced him to give way to Gladstone, leader of the new Liberal Party which had supplanted the Whigs as the main opposition to Disraeli's new Conservatives, who possessed views more progressive than those of the old-time Tories from whom they had evolved.

The Queen was charmed with Disraeli, who was accomplished as a courtier no less than as a statesman and a novelist; but she disliked Gladstone, whom she found lacking in tact—often awkward, generally unsympathetic, apparently hypocritical, always verbose. Both in speech and writing Gladstone seemed to be incapable of calling a spade a spade; he often lost himself in clouds of long words and tortuously formed sentences—a rhetorical trait that Victoria, forthright in word and deed, not unnaturally detested.

Solemnly earnest as well as incurably verbose, Gladstone lacked the sense of humor, cynical and playful, possessed by Disraeli. He was one of the greatest of the Victorian reformers, but unhappily he seemed to regard party politics as a religious crusade in which his own chosen side, whichever it happened to be (and he had been a Tory not so long ago, before changing to Liberalism), was the sole recipient of divine blessing and guidance.

Although Victoria was a sincerely religious woman, deeply attached to the Protestant cause, she found Gladstone's eternal self-righteousness a little tiring. He bored her, whereas Disraeli flattered and amused her.

When he was talking wittily to the poet Matthew Arnold one day, Disraeli said: "You have heard me called a flatterer, and it is true. Everyone likes flattery; and when you come to royalty you should lay it on with a trowel."

In another of his bright sayings he managed to crystallize into one short sentence the whole difference between him and his rival in their method of approach to Victoria whenever they had to explain to her any new measure they were introducing: "Gladstone treats the Queen like a public department; I treat her like a woman."

In his second term of office, lasting from 1874 to 1880, one form of flattery adopted by Disraeli was to link the Queen with himself on a literary level by occasionally addressing her as "We authors, Ma'am." It was a smiling allusion to the fact that Victoria had recently published, under the title of *Leaves from a Journal of Our Life in the Highlands,* a book giving extracts from the diary she had kept at Balmoral when Albert had been with her.

She was amused by Disraeli's tongue-in-cheek reference to "we authors," but she was not really deceived; she knew very well that her *Leaves,* an avowedly unpretentious volume, was far below the literary achievements of her clever Prime Minister. Beneath all the splendors of royalty—which she wore with increasing dignity during this prolonged golden sunset of her life—the Queen was innately modest, fully conscious of her own intellectual limitations when set beside the brilliant attainments of the many famous men and women of her reign.

That admirable trait of natural modesty had been well displayed in March of 1870, when, at her request, Charles Dickens visited Buckingham Palace. He was then engaged in writing *Edwin Drood,* the book he never finished; he was destined to die in June of that year. The royal command, the cherished summons to the admiring Queen's presence, therefore proved to be the final and crowning honor of his career.

In their long talk alone together, Victoria was enthralled to hear from his own lips the astonishing story of his life—blacking-factory to Buckingham Palace (by royal command)—and when at last she allowed him to depart she asked him to present her with signed copies of all his books. In return, she timidly handed to him an autographed copy of her published *Leaves,* bearing this inscription in her own hand: "From the humblest of writers to one of the greatest."

With the Queen for author, the *Leaves* not surprisingly had a big sale. The profit of £2,500 was used by her for founding scholarships for children of the Balmoral area. She never tired of visiting "our beloved Scotland," as she called her northern kingdom.

Balmoral Castle and Osborne House, both filled with memories of married happiness, were her favorite residences. She had never liked Buckingham Palace. As for Windsor—well, that was where Albert had died. Her frequent absences from London were a source of inconvenience to ministers, but Disraeli, for one, never openly grumbled at the long journeys often entailed when audiences were required.

The bestowal on Victoria of the title "Empress of India" in 1876 was the most glittering feature of Disraeli's second premiership. Henceforth the royal monogram "V.R." became "V.R.I.," signifying *Victoria Regina et Imperatrix*—"Victoria Queen and Empress." In gratitude she offered her Prime

Minister a peerage, which he accepted under the title of Earl of Beaconsfield.

For millions of Negro subjects in various parts of the world, especially Africa, Victoria had become "The Great White Queen," a distant and almost legendary figure of awe and majesty. No one had contributed more to that imperialistic conception than Lord Beaconsfield, who did not live long enough to see the celebrations of the fiftieth anniversary of her accession—the Golden Jubilee, as it was called.

Lord Salisbury, third marquis of that distinguished line, was then in Downing Street. The Queen soon found that she could place complete faith in his judgment, particularly in matters of foreign policy. His name became inseparably linked with the last phase of the Victorian era, and his various terms in the highest office under the crown were destined to exceed in total those of any other Prime Minister of the reign.

Lord Salisbury — tall, grave, dignified, dependable — was one of the most respected figures at the Golden Jubilee thanksgiving service in Westminster Abbey on June 21, 1887, when a galaxy of the crowned heads of Europe attended to pay honor to the Queen. After the excitements of a memorable day, she said on her return to Buckingham Palace, "I am very tired, but very happy."

The joy she felt on that occasion was easily eclipsed ten years later, on the occasion of the Diamond Jubilee; but in the meantime a date of signal importance to the history books had been reached and surpassed: on September 23,

1896, by then white-haired and sometimes compelled to use a wheel chair, the Queen became the longest-reigning monarch England had ever known, from the days of Alfred onward.

The previous record-holder had been George III, whose nominal reign had totaled fifty-nine years and ninety-six days, during much of which he had been incapacitated by recurring bouts of insanity. By contrast, no British monarch was ever saner—full of downright good sense to the very last—than Queen Victoria. Her increasing physical feebleness, mainly caused by rheumatism that made walking difficult, did not in the least affect her mind, which was alert and undimmed.

New marvels were still being invented, and she welcomed them with zest—apart from the horseless carriages, the rudimentary motor cars, which always seemed to be breaking down on the roads, and to which she never would entrust herself. But she was delighted to find that she could speak—if she wished—on the telephone from Windsor to Downing Street, and could hear in her drawing room the voice of Lord Tennyson booming out one of his poems on the new talking-machine, called phonograph, the grating father of the gramophone.

Photography had fascinated her from the start. In her old age she had an enormous collection of prints, most of them stiffly-posed portraits, typically Victorian, of young and old members of the ever-expanding family circle.

It was in 1896, on the occasion of a big family party at

Balmoral in celebration of the longest reign, that she personally participated in the latest marvel of all: the animated pictures. She and her guests, among them the Tsar Nicholas II of Russia, husband of one of her granddaughters, walked on the terrace while being "taken" by what the Queen called "the new cinematograph process, which takes moving pictures by winding off a reel of film."

The film was shown to her in a darkened room at Windsor later in the year. Everybody on the terrace, not excluding herself, seemed to be suffering from St. Vitus's Dance—an epidemic disease of the early cinema, which was invariably jumpy and jerky—but she was so delighted that she said it was "a wonderful process, representing people and their movements and actions as if they were alive."

At that happy family party on the terrace of Balmoral the Prince of Wales—"Bertie" to her—had been particularly tactful and gracious in his attentions on the Tsar and Tsarina (both doomed to be butchered in a cellar by Russian revolutionaries in 1918). As a consequence of his thoughtful conduct on that occasion, the Queen belatedly began to appreciate King Edward VII's abilities as an accomplished diplomatist. He was by then fifty-five years old, already a grandfather, but she had never allowed him to share as fully as he wished in affairs of state, apart from the purely decorative side.

It was a pity. But that was the way she was made: she liked power, and she kept most of it in her own hands to the last. The personal relations of·mother and son were nevertheless deeply affectionate at all times, and his reverence for her was intense. No one was prouder than he to witness the unprecedented demonstrations of loyalty given to his mother at the Diamond Jubilee celebrations, when millions of people lined six miles of London streets to cheer the Queen on her way to and from St. Paul's Cathedral, scene of the thanksgiving service.

Eight cream-colored horses drew the open landau on a day of blazing sunshine. It was June 22, 1897, two days after the actual sixtieth anniversary, which had fallen on a Sunday. The Queen—smiling happily but often near to tears on the triumphant and tumultuous journey—wore a dress of black silk trimmed with panels of grey satin and decorated on the front with gold embroidery worked in India. White flowers and a white aigrette adorned her black bonnet.

The service was in the open air, at the foot of the steps leading to the west door of the Cathedral. At Westminster Abbey ten years earlier there had been a great assemblage of foreign potentates, but for the Diamond Jubilee the main emphasis was on the Empire. Turbaned princes from India proudly stood near the carriage, and fifteen colonial Prime Ministers were in attendance.

The route from Buckingham Palace had been mainly through the wealthy West End of London, but meaner streets were deliberately chosen for the return. In the landau, which never exceeded walking-pace, Victoria crossed London Bridge and went back to the Palace through the teeming squalor of Southwark and Lambeth.

Yet "squalor" was hardly the word for that shining day. The faded streets had been transformed with flags everywhere, and the packed crowds roared their homage in an unbroken thunder of cheers. She had six solid miles of cheers on that great day. The return route was over Westminster Bridge, and at the palace that night the aged Queen, still faithful to the diary she had started as a little girl, made this entry:

> No one ever, I believe, has met with such an ovation as was given me, passing through those six miles of streets. The cheering was quite deafening, and every face seemed to be filled with real joy. I was much moved and gratified.

It was the summit of her glory. And it was set in a warming blaze of sunshine, with brilliantly fine weather for all the various jubilee celebrations held throughout the land during that joyful week. If she had died then, she would have died happy—in the full splendor of a golden sunset, before the dark.

That was not to be. Unhappily the remaining few years of the great reign were clouded by war: first in the Sudan and then in South Africa. The Queen's anxious care for the welfare of her troops engaged in those campaigns was unremitting, despite the fact that her eyesight was failing and she was finding much difficulty in reading all the many official documents submitted to her.

With the aid of secretaries she managed to maintain her

vigilant watch on affairs of state, and she was reassured to find that under the leadership of General Sir Herbert Kitchener, whom she rewarded with a peerage on his return, the Sudan expedition of 1898 was swiftly successful. Field Marshal Earl Kitchener of Khartoum, as he eventually became, also had a decisive part in the South African War, which began in the autumn of the following year and was still being waged when Victoria was stricken by her final illness on the threshold of the twentieth century.

In the early stages of that conflict the British forces suffered a series of humiliating defeats during the closing weeks of 1899, in consequence of which Lord Roberts, accompanied by Kitchener as Chief-of-Staff, was sent out to take supreme command. In the dark phase the Queen was never a defeatist, unlike some of her ministers, to one of whom she said: "Please understand that there is no one depressed in my house. We are not interested in the possibilities of defeat. They do not exist."

She lived long enough to see the turn of the tide, with the main strength of the enemy broken by the ruthless campaigns of 1900; and at Osborne, in January of 1901, she was able to welcome Lord Roberts on his return from the front, where only mopping-up operations were required. She gave several audiences to him, but it was evident that her strength was failing fast. The truth was that she was physically worn out.

"What news from Lord Kitchener?" was her first and only question to Lord Roberts at the final audience. That was the last coherent sentence she ever spoke. Realizing that the end was near, her family had been gathering round her at Osborne, and on the 19th an official bulletin announced that the Queen was suffering from "physical prostration."

Death came at six-thirty in the evening on January 22, 1901. Next day the newspapers of the land were heavily edged in black, and the whole world went into mourning. Her age was eighty-one years and eight months, and the reign had lasted sixty-three years, seven months, and two days. She had lived three days longer than George III, the longest-lived British sovereign hitherto, and her reign had exceeded his by nearly four years.

For a few days before being transferred to the mainland in a warship, the body lay in state in the dining room of Osborne. One of her last wishes had been that no black trappings should be near her in death. For nearly forty years she had been in mourning, but for this final scene the drapings round the white coffin were of crimson and ermine, not sable. Over her face lay her wedding veil, put there at her special request.

Thus she was placed beside Albert in the royal mausoleum of Frogmore in the grounds of Windsor Castle. Victoria had given her name to an illustrious era, and all the people mourned. It was the end of an epoch, a proud period of British history.

Index of People and Places

142